HUSH TO ROAR

To my dearest ones who have given me purpose:

In loving memory of my foster dad, Mr Ernest Kind. Dad, you took me in and loved me no matter what! I miss you.

In loving memory of my fondest and most-loving foster sister, Carolyn Sperry. I will always love you. You got sent from above, you were my angel and you knew I had to start my early life with your family. I miss you.

In loving memory of Grandmum and Grandpa Kind. You provided me with an extra layer of love and cushioned me with emotional stability in the most crucial years of my life. I love and miss you.

In loving memory of my stepdad: Dad, I will always be your little girl. I miss you.

My foster mum, Mrs Shirley Kind: Mum, you wrapped me in your arms. I always felt your tenderness, even when I wasn't with you. I love you. You are my rainbow.

My foster siblings: Julie, Andrew and Paula, thank you for immersing me in love.

All my half-siblings, seventeen of you: thank you for being integral in my journey and making me laugh.

My birth mum: Without you I would not be here. You've worked hard all your life, and strived tirelessly to provide for us all. You did the best you knew how. Thank you.

My biological father: I will always give you the love that incorporates compassion.

My husband: you helped me see the imperfections that have fuelled me to become a better person. Thank you for cooking the most delicious and nutritious traditional soups and teaching our children how to cook when I had my head buried in the writing of this book.

My precious jewels, my children: I got the privilege to have you in my care. Thanks for loving me even when I get it wrong. Thank you for being my cheerleaders in all I lay my hands on. I promise to continue to be your champion and give it my all to be the loving and patient mum that you deserve.

Disclaimer: Some names and identifying details of people described in this book have been altered to protect their privacy.

ISBN: 978-1-8381533-3-5

CONTENTS

PART I: A Nurtured Child

PART II: Over and Over

PART III: Life Promises Life

PART IV: Healing

PART I

A NURTURED CHILD

CHAPTER 1

Carolyn

Little did she know that her persistence on this day would be the most significant, life-saving thing she would ever do.

'Mum, you've got to see this.'

'Mum, you're not listening.'

'You've got to see this.'

Carolyn cried out again after Mum, who was preoccupied with the dinner. But, this time, she was determined to get Mum's attention. She'd seen an advertisement in the newspaper she had picked up from the local newsstands for Dad early that morning, before heading off to school.

My foster dad, I was told, couldn't do without the morning newspapers on the breakfast table. He would intermittently sip his hot tea while he read them.

An advert posted in the papers for the foster care of a little black girl had caught Carolyn's attention that morning. She'd flipped through the pages to see if there was anything of interest to her. The advertisement read:

I would like a loving family to foster my black baby. If you are the perfect family, please write your number and your address on the brown envelope enclosed, and post it to the address below.

When Carolyn got back from school, she was so excited to see the morning paper still lying on the small side table. It sat neatly on its own, on the shiny, well-polished table that Mum so often cleaned with such pride.

'Carolyn, dear, what is so important that can't wait?' Mum said, while still trying to set some dishes on the table. 'There's so much to do, and your dad will soon be home for dinner.'

'I know, Mum, but you've got to see this.'

Carolyn flicked through the pages to get to the advertisement seeking the foster care of a black baby girl. She set it on the dining table for Mum to read. That little girl was me. It was October 1972, and I was just two months old.

Mum – my white foster mum – would always recall how Carolyn was like a 'dog with a bone'; she just wouldn't let it go when it came to this advertisement.

She said, 'Carolyn went on and on about this baby girl, and she wouldn't stop until we responded to the advert asking us to send our phone number to an address by post if we were interested in fostering their baby. Ooh, Bas, you were her favourite, and she was fond of you, you know? God bless her sweet soul now.'

Mum Kind exhaled a silent breath, as she held my hands firmly. She reflected on how, if it were not for Carolyn, I would not have come into her life.

Carolyn's persistence for Mum to respond to the advert resulted in the most significant moment of my life.

'Mum, let's give it a go.'

Mum was not sure what it would be like to raise a black child in a completely white village. 'Carolyn, dear, I'm not so sure. I've never seen a coloured baby in Ratby before.'

'I know, Mum. Let's reply to the post; nothing will probably come of it. Let's do it for fun.'

'All right, Carolyn, let's do it. But Dad doesn't have to know since nothing will come of it, right?'

'OK, Mum,' Carolyn said. 'Let's do it.'

It was around 6 pm and just over a week since Mum and Carolyn had replied to the advert.

'Get the phone, please, darling,' Dad called out to Mum when the phone rang.

'Hello.'

'Hello, you said you want to foster my baby?'

Mum cringed a bit in surprise, almost not sure of what to say.

'Ehhhm, hold on a minute, please...' Placing her hand on the mouthpiece, she leaned over to Dad. 'Ern [short for my foster dad's name – Ernest] I've got this lady on the phone asking if we'll foster her baby. What should I tell her?'

'What are you talking about?' Dad replied with a puzzled look on his face.

Mum told him she and Carolyn had responded to the advert in the *Leicester Mercury* newspaper, not expecting a response.

After a puzzled thirty seconds, Dad simply shrugged his shoulders and said, 'I don't know. I guess we'll have to. I don't know.' Dad smiled and looked at Mum. 'You've applied to have her, so yes, I guess we'll have to do the right thing and have her.'

That was my foster dad; he was someone who firmly believed that once you have given your word, you've got to keep it.

Without any other thought, and being mindful that she'd had the lady on the phone for a few minutes now, Mum muttered, 'Sorry to keep you waiting. Yes, we would love to foster your baby.'

Before Mum could ask for more details, my birth mum, relieved and excited to have found someone willing to help take care of me, hurriedly said, 'Thank you. See you, thank you very much...' and hung up the phone.

CHAPTER 2

A Black Baby

Mum told me about the very first time they went to pick me up from my biological family. My foster parents both peered to see me as I snuggled into my birth mum's arms, clutching her firmly and leaning my head inwards towards her chest.

'Her name is "Basirat",' my birth mum said. 'It means 'happiness'. It's a Nigerian Muslim name.'

'Baa..sh..rat,' Mum and Dad struggled in unison.

Dad quickly said, 'Bas! We'll call her Bas for short. I hope that's OK?'

My birth mum replied, 'Of course, whatever you feel comfortable with.'

They had a long chat about my sleep routine and other necessary information. My birth mum served some drinks, seizing the opportunity to get to know them a little bit more in a short space of time. She then proceeded to hand over bags to my foster parents, finishing off by saying, 'I'll speak to you about the weekly allowance and how we can arrange for her to come over once or twice a month at the weekends.'

Trying very hard not to look surprised that I would be with them from that night onwards, Mum and Dad replied, 'Yes, yes, of course.'

Mum said my birth mum was clearly trying not to cry and, without further conversation, quickly put my pink knitted woollen hat on me, buttoning up the matching cardigan. She was sure my biological mum said the unspoken words, 'Please take care of my baby.'

She responded out loud, 'We'll take great care of her, Wasi [my birth mum's name, short for Wasilat].'

Mum said when my biological mother handed me to her, she could see she had glistening teary eyes. Apparently I screamed my head off. While rocking me gently in her arms, she kissed me on the forehead.

'We'll take care of you, me duck.'

In the early 1970s, the UK had no legislation in place for this type of fostering; as to how babies or children were fostered or, indeed, what process should take place. It was very lackadaisical; a somewhat laid-back approach to care arrangements was taken. There were no social workers or paperwork. As I was growing up with my foster parents a formal process of fostering was just beginning to be introduced. My birth parents and foster parents came up with their own arrangements. These included regular visits to see my biological family, which took place once, or sometimes twice, every month. An allowance to be paid to my foster parents was agreed between my biological parents and foster parents.

My foster mum recalled how she couldn't keep her eyes off me on the drive to their home. She said I soon settled down in the car and my smile was infectious.

Dad had barely opened the front door when my four foster siblings – Julie, Andrew, Carolyn and Paula – rushed downstairs, hardly feeling the stairs beneath their feet. They all assembled around Mum, each one reaching to see me as I moved my head back and forth, trying to get glimpses of all four of them.

Julie, the eldest, was thirteen when I joined their family at two months old. Andrew was next, at eleven years old, then Carolyn, who was nine. Paula was the last born until I came along. She was the closest in age to me even though there was a five-year gap between us.

'Awwww, she's lovely,' Carolyn said, smiling and kissing my little hand. 'She's tiny! I love her already! How old is she, Mum?'

'She's two months old,' Mum said.

Mum got everyone to sit down so I wouldn't get frightened.

'That's right, everyone, let's go and sit down comfortably.'

As the children settled down and began to talk excitedly amongst themselves about the new addition to their family, Mum suddenly turned to Dad.

'Ern! How are we going to let everyone see Bas?'

'What do you mean?' Dad replied.

'Well, there's no coloured baby in Ratby, is there? And people might stare and ask awkward questions. How should we introduce her? So that we'll be prepared for people before they ask questions when I go out with her?'

She told me that even though she and Carolyn had mentioned the possible awkwardness of having a black baby in a predominately white village before placing the advert, the reality suddenly kicked in.

Before Dad could reply, she exclaimed, 'I know! Why don't we take her to the Garden Show, when you play in your band on Saturday? You know how tight-knit the village is. Everyone's always in everyone's business, and they'll be wondering where the heck we found a coloured baby. If we take her to the Garden Show, the whole village can say what they want to say to us out in the open. They can ask us questions once and for all and start to become comfortable seeing her out and about.'

Her plan sure did work, and it worked a treat! From that day onward, it felt like the whole of Ratby loved me.

As a toddler, and before I started school, I was my foster mum's 'handbag'. I was ubiquitous. Wherever she turned, there I was.

My foster mum would take me with her to work, where she did the cleaning at the school I eventually attended. Using my little bucket and mop, I would mop where she'd already cleaned and get in her way. Mum would simply say, 'Oh, Bas, that's enough now.'

Our house in Ratby was situated right next to the beautiful woods, Martin Shaw Woods. Once I was around five, I would dash off into the woods on my own at times; it was my friendly forest of fun. I loved rushing off to Martin Shaw Forest. My brother and sisters would call out to me to stay and finish reading to them. I'd say, 'Love you, see you later.'

I knew Martin Shaw Forest would greet me with the swaying of the leaves on the trees. The sun broke through the cracks, lighting up the dirt path for me. I felt the fallen leaves crunch beneath my feet. I got greeted by my friends, the bright-coloured, shy yet bold bullfinches. They were broad-chested, and confident in their beauty. I yearned to see them but was mostly only greeted by their sweet singing, soft piping note, saying (or so I thought), 'Hi, Bas.'

One day Mum was with me in the woods, as we'd both gone for a walk. I twirled along while gazing up at the trees, tracing the sweet singing tunes of the bullfinch birds. I called them my forest friends.

'Mum! Hurry, Mum, they're calling me,' I said, pulling her along as we followed the sound further into the woods. I ploughed on, taking in the fragrance of the minty grass and damp earth so that I could get a glimpse of the birds.

'Here, Mum!'

'Oh, Bas, you have to be still. They're shy, me duck.'

Mum made sure I was quiet enough not to scare them away. With some luck, we eventually saw a pair of brightly coloured bullfinches. I stood still once I caught a glimpse, and so did Mum.

'Sshhhh…not a word now, Bas,' she said quietly, pulling me closer.

We watched on, hoping they'd stay. But as soon as we were spotted, the birds hopped two branches away and tweeted a couple of times. Then they flew away – but this time deeper into the woods, so they soon disappeared out of sight.

When I was on my own, I played in my den and made mud pies, and I would go bluebell picking. I would give them to Mum, kissing her hurriedly and rushing back out again.

I loved watching my forest friends in their element. I would watch the squirrels climb up the trees as though they had scheduled to be somewhere soon; it was one of my unique places to be, to feel the fullness of life, wholesomely.

Mum shaped me and nurtured me in a way that helped me explore the world safely and securely. Her love for nature was indicative of how she reflected on her world. As I grew older, the hums of the forest brought alive in me the same appreciation of nature. I played there for hours on end. I was only reminded that it was time to say goodbye to my forest friends when the sun said goodbye to me first. Then I'd dash home for supper.

Mum's meals were always superb. Dinner times also brought us closer together as a family.

'Supper's ready!' Mum would call out.

On the table would sit bowls of chicken stew. She often used the chicken carcass left over from the Sunday roast and turned it into a casserole. She was very resourceful and economical.

We'd all sit around the table, waiting for the first person to speak. Often it would be Dad or me, and others joined in as we devoured the delicious meals.

I loved standing at the kitchen door, with my toes pointing outwards, and tilting back and forth. I enjoyed the cool breeze when it was windy or raining. I'd lean outside in the rain until I landed out in the showers, and Mum would say, 'Bas, come inside quickly. You've got soaked now.'

In an earnest tone, with my hands spread out, I'd reply, 'The wind blew me out.'

Mum would laugh hysterically, pulling me in as she shut the door behind me.

No doubt there must have been times when I got told off at Ratby, but I certainly have no memories of ever being overly upset about anything in particular.

Our eldest sister, Julie, was simply 'big sis'. She was there for me like a 'little mum' when Mum was out somewhere. My fondest memory of Julie was when I was her flower girl in 1979. I can't express how ecstatic I was. I could barely sleep the night before.

Julie was twenty, and it was her wedding day on 17th March 1979. I was seven years old. Mum dressed me up in a gorgeous warm red felt dress that had quarter-arm lengths of white fluffy, feathery edges. I felt like I was wearing warm snow that didn't melt. I wore a white cosy feathery hat with silky ribbons attached that Mum tied in a bow. She made sure it was nice and firm on my head. My shoes were out of this world! They were a lovely pair of high patent burgundy shoes with a high gloss finish. I remember slipping them on and walking with such elegance. Before it was time to leave for the church service, I opened the door and stuck out my tongue to feel the gentle lush, powdery heavenly beauty. I looked up to the sky to see the clouds break into a deluge of whirling snow. It was a perfect day for my gorgeous sister to get married. Large flakes fell as if angels in Heaven were having a pillow fight.

We stepped out to leave, and I remember holding up my long dress slightly. The wind whispered as the snow fell like confetti on my hat. The ground was as smooth as the wedding cake I was anticipating. The snow fell soundlessly like blankets of icing powder. Once we got in the car, Mum kept looking back at me to make sure my hat covered my ears, because though the snow was beautiful, it was freezing. That day remains one of my most memorable days as a child, as the flower girl at Julie's wedding.

I loved playing with my brother and sisters; being the baby of the house was lovely. They all made me feel special in their unique ways.

Andrew was my darling big brother. I recall one day going to his room to call him for something, and he wasn't there. As soon as I popped my head in, I remember screaming and everyone running upstairs to see what the matter was. A big Dracula picture was on his wall with blood dripping out of its mouth. I was petrified! That was the first and last time I went into his room.

Above left: Me, Paula and Carolyn on Julie's wedding day in 1979.
Above right: Me and Paula in a school photo.

I can't begin to describe the bond I had with Carolyn. She was the fondest sister ever. She loved taking me to the sweet shop with her. I'd do something silly and Carolyn would say, 'Oh, Bas, you're my cutest sister ever. What would I do without you?'

Even though Paula was the closest to me in age, we were in the same school for just a year due to the age gap. Everyone knew us as sisters, and I would take school photos with her, snuggling up to her and leaning on her proudly, as if to say, 'There's my big sis.'

We all enjoyed Bonfire Night where we cooked spuds in the fire, but Christmas was always the best. I would start my Christmas holidays with Mum's friend Lil, who took me to visit every single Santa's grotto, without fail, over my entire childhood in Ratby. She was so sweet. I'd hold her hand tightly as we approached the Grotto. As I was the only black child in the village, I'm sure it wasn't difficult for Santa to know my name. My grin was ear to ear. I always felt extra special that he'd see me and say, 'Ho ho ho, hello, Bas.'

He'd pat his lap as I walked up to him, half scared and half excited. Once I was comfortable on his lap, I would tilt my head slightly to gaze at his long white cotton beard. He spoke as if he controlled the world, and his voice rumbled like a storm deep inside of him as he hummed the 'Jingle Bells' tune. He'd ask me if I'd been a good girl, I'd nod and say, 'Yes, I've been a good girl.' His baritone voice reverberated through my bones. It was a voice with authority as a kindly laugh shook the ground like a snowstorm.

On Christmas Days, Mum would serve the most delicious homemade trifles. Growing up, I would liken the table of food to that out of a scene from *Alice in Wonderland*. It was always a table full of bright-coloured, delightful dishes. Mum would slice up the jam-and-cream swiss rolls, layer them at the bottom of a big Pyrex dish, top it up with fruit, jelly and grated chocolate and ask me to spoon whipped cream on top of it. It was such a treat. I would leave some cream on the spoon and lick it off, smiling at Mum cheekily. Then I would watch Mum melt the jelly in a jug of hot water. Before she tossed it all in, I'd quickly say, 'Mum! Wait! Please don't melt all the jelly.' She'd cut off a square and pop it in my mouth.

Each spoonful of her delicious trifle would have me in total bliss at the dinner table. I would be rubbing my foot, one resting on top of the other, while humming sounds that meant nothing to others, but every single hum was full of lovely trifle that melted in my mouth.

We would sometimes go to my birth mum's house to spend Christmas. Enjoying the delicacy my biological mum had made, I would often ask to have a tiny sip of Babycham. A small drop got dotted on my tongue, and I would ask why I couldn't have a lot more. They'd say it was a special drink for adults, but I would shake my head saying, 'It's for a child, that's why it has the baby deer on it.'

When it was time for dessert, my birth mum brought a delicious-looking cake to the table. Mum took a bite of the cake. It was frozen! My birth mum hadn't realised it should have been defrosted first, because it looked exactly like fluffy ice cream. Everyone was in stitches, laughing hysterically.

Pets were a big part of the family, ranging from owls to parrots to different breeds of dogs, including Newfoundlands and Chihuahuas. I was most fond of our big Newfoundlands, Beaulah and Elsa. Even though they were big dogs, both Elsa and Beaulah were like giant teddies. They were intelligent and strong, like gentle giants. The breed are working dogs for fishermen in Newfoundland, Canada. Newfoundlands are swim dogs and used as rescue dogs. As swim dogs, Beaulah and Elsa were often in competitions, and I remember when Beaulah won a bike as part of the prizes. The red Raleigh bike we won became mine, and I rode it everywhere.

Mum would send me on errands on my bike, to buy cake ingredients. I would get home with smashed eggs, mixed in with the flour, and a slimy tub of butter. With her eyes raised to the ceiling, and shaking her head, she'd say, 'Oh, Bas, all we need to do is pop it all in the oven. You've already mixed up all the ingredients.' I would say sorry and run off to play without a care in the world.

At the weekends, I would go to see my biological family maybe once or twice a month, dragging my foster sister Carolyn to a sleepover with me. My biological sister was born when I turned three and she was at a different foster home, my brothers were, six, nine and twelve years old. Our parents ensured we had the same visiting times so we could meet up at home. Once my biological brothers were old enough to stay at home, they no longer went to their foster family. Carolyn, my little sister and I slept on freshly made beds, with talcum powder all over the bed sheets. We'd wake up puffed in powder; my birth mum would laugh and say she'd sprinkled the powder on to keep us smelling fresh. She would wash and plait my hair, and we'd go back home on a Sunday afternoon. I loved seeing my little sister, when she was a bit older we'd play with our Sindy dolls together for hours on end. When it was time to leave, and my foster dad had come to pick Carolyn and me up, my

Above: Me and Carolyn (inseparable! With our matching outfits), getting dropped off to spend the weekend with my biological family.

big brothers would throw me up in the air and give me a bear hug. I'd hug my little sister and kiss her goodbye, knowing that I'd see her in a short while. We would both wear our hair in the same way.

Looking after an African hair type was undoubtedly difficult for my foster mum. She often struggled with my hair, especially trying to figure out how to undo the plaits my birth mum had made. Mum would take out the braids once they started to get untidy and comb my hair, leaving me with an afro that she could manage better.

My foster dad held me dear in his heart – I was his little Bas. I would watch him play the trumpet in his band on Saturdays if I didn't go to my biological family. We'd get back from the Garden Show and Dad would have a snooze on the settee. I would seize this opportunity to play over his legs. I hopped back and forth with a long broom as I sang the Halloween song, 'Ho ho ho…and the witch came riding by'. I had absolute freedom to play and be a little girl.

Even though I was growing up as a free-spirited little girl, my foster parents instilled good manners in us all and taught us always to be courteous and kind to others, remembering to be humble at all times.

Most of my summer holidays with my foster family were spent visiting my foster grandparents in Torquay. Dad would drive us from Leicester to Torquay; it took us about four hours, clocking up around 209 miles. Although the landscape throughout the journey along the countryside was fun to look at, for a little girl, nothing compared to when we finally got closer to the coastline of the town itself. Its clear sky, calm beaches and the hills and mountains outlining some of its beautiful harbours were fascinating to me. As we entered the town, driving along its coastline, my foster siblings and I would get excited, and the sea air and chilled atmosphere greeted us.

The fun at home with my foster grandparents was unique. I recall how Grandpa would roughen my hair up with some vigour. He called me Daz. This was from the washing powder; he would say I needed a scrub. I'd chase him around the garden, then he'd make a quick turn and start running after me.

I would get exhausted and then go to Grandma for some Pops cherryade. I loved watching her bake my favourite iced tart. She'd simply place a layer of pastry on a large rectangular baking tray, spread some jam on top, put another pastry layer over the jam and pop it in the oven.

I would potter about waiting for the tart to bake. As soon as it was ready, Grandmum would help me up on a stepping stool to mix the icing, and I would spoon it all over the pastry and wait anxiously for this divine iced tart to be ready. She would cut a little slice for me and I would run off to meet up with my brother and sisters on the beach.

It was such fun on the beach. I made sandcastles and enjoyed candy floss and ice cream. I would copy my foster mum and my sisters as they lay down to sunbathe, not that I needed a tan.

Top left : Me chasing Grandad Kind.
Top right: Grandad Kind carrying me and our dog, Rusty.
Bottom left: Grandmum carrying me.
Bottom right: Me at two in Grandad and Grandmum's beautiful garden.

Top left: Me and mum on the beach.
Top right: Me and mum.
Bottom left, from left: Carolyn, me holding our dog, Paula behind me; and Julie.
Bottom right: Dad Kind, grandad, me and grandmum.

My foster siblings and I would play on the beach, enjoying the feel of the white, powdery sand that held us up as we stepped on it. The warmth beneath my feet felt friendly.

After spending ample time on the beach, we'd go back to the holiday home where Grandmum would have made a delicious dish of roasted vegetables and potatoes, served with chicken thighs and plenty of gravy. I always looked forward to this and impatiently waited for the delightful iced tart for dessert.

I received high-level genuine love, mental and emotional stability, and care at a very young age from my foster family. I was a little smiling girl of great independence. I was free to communicate my feelings, and I had a real sense of security within me.

CHAPTER 3

Our Bas

My experience at school was a beautiful and memorable one. I made so many friends and felt so much warmth from the community as a whole. I felt no differentiation as the only black child in the school of around 360 pupils. It was quite incredible.

My best friend's name was Kerry; my two other closest friends were Joanne and Tracey. Kerry lived just across the road from me. I often went to her house to play on the slide. We played on the swing in her garden. When we finished at hers, we'd rush over to my house. Mum would have Heinz Sandwich Spread ready for us – a blend of salad cream with finely diced carrots, celery, gherkins, red peppers and mustard. We'd both gobble up the sandwiches so we could dash off to Martin Shaw Woods to go bluebell picking.

The sea of the bluebells in the woods was simply a thing of beauty. Kerry and I would play there, making mud pies and playing hide and seek as we listened to the sweet singing birds and the scuffling squirrels.

When we weren't in the woods, we would have our other friends Joanne and Tracey join us. We would play with marbles on top of round drain covers in the streets, or play 'Elastic'. This was a game with a long piece of elastic, tied in a loop around the ankles of two players, with a third person jumping over it. The elastic is raised to knees and then to the waist.

The four of us would talk about our teachers and how we were all scared of the dinner lady. Some days I'd go to the fish and chip shop with Dad. I'd plead to go with him so that I could play with Joanne, as her family owned it. Joanne and I would play in the shop as Dad waited for our fish and chips, mushy peas and gherkins.

School was fun. I'd walk past the sweet shop on the way to school, eyes glued to the window where the halfpenny sweets were on display. My favourite ones were Fruit Salads, Black Jacks, Dip Dab Sherbets, and Marathon [now called Snickers] chocolate bars.

During assembly, we would sing the 'Building Song': 'Everybody's building, everybody's building day by day...everybody's building in a different way'. The song would be on a projector, and one of our teachers would play the guitar.

Afterwards, we'd all wait patiently for our milk that was served every day, in a glass bottle. The bottle felt warm in the summer and ice cold in the winter. It was so refreshing and travelled straight to my brain. It was as if that was the plan, to wake us up and make us be attentive in class.

We would have sewing lessons and read the Billy Blue Hat and Janet and John books. I loved reading; it was my absolute favourite thing to do. I stood up confidently in class. Our teacher would say, 'Bas, are you ready? Off you go.' I was expressive with every word I said. I'd read and smile, at times taking it slow and glancing at my friends to see if they were giggling.

I chuckle now remembering bizarre things that happened. Once we found a handprint on the door like a scene from a horror film, and a hot rumour started going round that it was made by a ghost. It was one of those incidents that as a six- or seven-year-old you believed, and nothing could convince you otherwise. We'd all say we had to be well behaved, otherwise the ghost might come and take us away.

School dinners were also exciting times. Sitting at the tables were glasses of water, and at the bottom of these glasses was a number that determined how old you were. We had a variety of dinners, such as cheese pie, chicken fricassee, sponge puddings and coloured custard. The pink one was my absolute favourite. I'd want to rush for seconds, but would wait for my friends if they hadn't finished so we could all go together because we were scared of the dinner lady. We'd all scoop up our preferred coloured custard and go out to play.

We'd run to our favourite spot on the playground. My friends and I would stand and decide which game to play first. All of us would shout out our favourite game. Sometimes it would be a quick game or two of hopscotch – jumping into a chalked square on the floor. Each one of us would take turns to hop into and over the squares marked on the floor and pick up a marker thrown into one of them. We'd carefully bend down to get it. If your foot touched the line, you'd be out.

After a few games of hopscotch and leapfrogs, we'd be exhausted and sit down. We'd each choose our partner. I'd usually be with my best friend, Kerry. We'd play clapping rhymes. This was another one of my favourite games. Our default rhyme would almost always be:

'A sailor went to sea sea sea
To see what he could see see see
But all that he could see see see
Was the bottom of the deep blue sea sea sea.'

We'd clap faster and faster, rhyming and bursting with laughter. We felt our heads racing as we sang the rhyme. We wouldn't stop until our hands got hot and tired.

Maypole dancing was part of our fun things to do in May. There would be a pole in the middle with long drapes of colourful ribbons that we all danced around. Sometimes we'd get tangled up in them.

In September, we had Harvest Festivals, and our parents would give us tins of food to take to church. We felt very proud and happy that our cans of food would feed the hungry.

Christmas dinners were impressive; the whole school atmosphere felt Christmassy. We would take in Christmas wrapping paper to cover our desks when we had a Christmas buffet in class.

Above: Me and my classmates in an Easter Bonnet picture.

I recall when my class teacher said I was going to be an angel during one of the Christmas plays. With a big smile on my face, I rushed home. I couldn't wait to tell everyone. I rushed over to Mum and Dad, full of smiles. I shouted with excitement, 'Mum, Dad, I'm going to be an angel for our Christmas play.'

Mum said, 'That's lovely, Bas.'

Dad turned to look at us and said in a loving tone, 'Who's ever seen a coloured angel?'

Mum, with a big smile on her face, said, 'We have, our Bas.'

Dad said, 'Come here, Bas.' He patted his lap.

I ran and jumped on him, saying, 'Yes, Dad, I am your angel, and you'll see me as an angel at school.'

Dad said, 'Ouch, Bas.' He snuggled his head in my belly and gave me a raspberry kiss, leaving me laughing hysterically on the floor.

For the Christmas school play Mum dressed me up in a long white dress and a silver glistering tiara.

After school, I'd go knocking on our neighbour's house. Her name was Ena, and she was an elderly lady who lived on her own, so I'd go to keep her company. I'd flip off my shoes and put them neatly, just as Ena liked them, in a corner. I'd start chatting away to her as she baked lemon and strawberry tarts; she'd wash my hands and wipe my face as we waited for the baked pies. Once they were ready, we'd sit and talk for ages. Ena would tell me about what she'd been doing during the day, like knitting hats that she'd take to the Garden Show on Saturdays. She would ask me what I'd been up to at school, saying she knew I was a good girl and she hoped I'd played nicely. Once I'd finished at Ena's, I'd be so full from having lots of tarts that I sometimes skipped supper at home.

I was simply at ease with myself. All those around me filled me with confidence and the self-belief that made a very jolly and a happy little Bas, beaming brightly with laughter. I was always known to be that little girl who smiled ear to ear. I never once thought that I was being fostered. I knew my biological parents were indeed my parents; I also had no doubt that my mum and dad Kind, siblings and Grandma and Grandpa in Torquay were always going to be in my life. I always knew, in my heart, that I'd live with them for ever!

CHAPTER 4

Inconsolable

It was a summery day towards the end of August. We had got back from Torquay just a week earlier. The warm air and the beautiful, blazing bloom of flowers with the smell of pink petals were all around. As I played outside, I thought of my school friends that I would be seeing in the next two weeks after a long, lovely summer holiday. I had just turned eight in August 1980.

'Bas!' Mum called out.

I ran to her as usual.

'Are you alright, love?'

'Yes, Mum. Are you OK?'

'Yes, me love,' she replied. 'Come on in, The *Little House on the Prairie* is about to start.'

I loved watching this American western historical drama series, and I particularly enjoyed watching the three girls tumble down the hill at the start of the drama. The youngest was a cutie.

I squeezed past Mum in a hurry and took my position right in between my two sisters, Carolyn and Paula. I usually loved watching the intro more than the actual programme itself. Mum took a glance at me. As soon as she saw that I had lost interest at the end of the programme, she said, 'Bas, come here a minute.'

She wasn't her usual smiling self.

'Sit here,' she said, patting her lap.

Usually when I tried to sit on her lap she'd laugh about how I was getting heavier, but this time was different. I sat firmly on her lap. She took a deep breath as if she wanted to get something off her chest. I felt a sudden silence from everyone. It was strange because Dad and all my siblings were present but it was so quiet.

'Bas, Wasi will be coming to pick you up in a few days.'

She was referring to my biological mum. Before she could finish, I butted in, jumped off her lap, and shouted, 'Can Carolyn come with me? Please, please, please.'

Mum looked at me, but almost immediately looked to the floor, shaking her head slowly.

'No, darling, Carolyn can't come with you. Wasi is taking you to Nigeria. You won't be coming back to us.'

I remember looking into her eyes and seeing them glitter. I could feel the tears in her eyes for me, just as she felt them herself. I stood stiff and heard sniffles from my brother and sisters. Paula got up and hugged me as I said nothing. Before I knew it, I felt arms all around me. My siblings were around me, except Carolyn. They all started to sob. They were hugging me, but I stood still. I was in pain. It felt like the pain of an immunisation needle running through my whole body. I reached out to my foster mum, saying, 'No, no, no.' I hugged her tightly. Once my first tear broke free, the rest followed in an unbroken stream. I could taste the continuous flow of salty taste of tears seep uncontrollably into the corners of my mouth. I said nothing. I could say nothing. I was inconsolable.

I felt oxygen leave my throat. I was gasping for air. I felt like my world was crashing down on me. All my emotions were racing at once.

Mum hugged me tight; she felt what I felt and fought back her emotions. She was just as inconsolable as I was.

I looked to Carolyn; she had her head in her hands, sobbing uncontrollably. I turned around, looking to my foster dad.

'Will I never see Carolyn, Julie, Paula and Andrew ever again?' I asked in a shaky voice. 'Will I never see you and Mum again? So I won't see Grandma and Grandpa in Torquay ever again? I won't see Kerry and my other friends ever again?'

I'm sure Mum hoped some magical fairy would answer those questions favourably for me, just as she wanted for herself.

Articulating what I was hearing felt impossible. Just a few minutes before, I had been thinking about how I would finish watching *Little House on the Prairie* and run to my neighbour friend to keep her company. I had been thinking of how Kerry, Joanne, Tracey and I would chatter on about our summer holidays when we went back to school. We would be talking about our new school year and teachers, hoping that they wouldn't take the pink custard off the school menu.

I couldn't believe I was leaving Ratby.

I was about to ask another question when Dad got up from the settee and picked me up. Hugging me and fighting back his tears, he said, 'You will see us all again.'

He tried to reassure me that I would be back. I looked him in the eye and said, 'Dad, do you promise?'

He lowered me to the floor and got on his knees, down to my level. He paused with a heavy sigh, hugging me tightly again, and quietly said, 'I promise, Bas.'

It seemed like my foster mum informed them about me leaving in one minute and, a minute later, I got picked up. It all happened so quickly.

It was fun spending time with my biological family when I went over once or twice a month for the weekend, but I couldn't imagine life without my foster family and friends.

I never did go back to school in the first week of September, as anticipated. I contracted chicken pox. No one could come to see me due to the highly contagious nature of the illness. My best friend Kerry and my close friends, Joanne and Tracey, didn't see me leave, and I couldn't go to my elderly neighbour friend. I didn't say goodbye to Grandma and Grandpa Kind in Torquay. I never got to see them again.

I hoped Mum would say, 'It's OK, Bas, Wasi is not taking you to Nigeria anymore.' That was never the case.

It was time for me to go to my biological family, although I had grown up with my foster family, and I thought I would always be with them.

When it was time to say goodbye to my foster family, I couldn't utter a word. It felt like a sharp object had pierced my heart. I felt like the blood in my veins was frozen. I said nothing. Mum hugged me tightly and I felt tears roll down my face uncontrollably. It all seemed like a blur.

She and Dad gave me a final hug, and I quickly ran to my brother and sisters for one more hug. I held them tight, tugging at them. I pulled them side to side. I didn't utter any audible words. My throat felt tight.

As we hugged, they all said, 'We'll write loads of letters to you every day. We'll tell you about every little or big thing that we're getting up to. You will always feel like you're still with us. Make sure you write to us too!'

'I'll write you two letters every day,' I said, tears still flowing down my cheeks.

They all sang the 'Brotherhood of Man' (winners of Eurovision Song contest in 1976) song in unison: 'Save all your kisses for me'.

Mum took my hand and walked me to the car. I looked back at my foster family, holding each other's hands tightly. Tears ran down their cheeks as they tried to sing the song to me. I looked up to Mum, and she whisked me up from the floor, holding me tight. I didn't want her to let go.

My birth mum and dad stood near the car. They waved at my foster family and then opened the door for me to get in the back seat. I got in, knelt facing backwards and looked through the windscreen. I swayed from side to side, a lonely and heartbroken slow-motion wave.

My little hand made a continuous screeching sound on the windscreen. Tears streamed down my face. I watched them all get smaller and smaller as we drove away. I saw them fade away gradually into tiny images until I could see them no more.

As my birth dad drove, there was silence. I stared out of the window, looking at the swaying trees and thinking they were just as sad as I was. I wondered if they were sorry that I was leaving Ratby.

It was late summer. The earth was ready for the rains, for sweet drops to quench the soils. I imagined the pitter-patter returning to the Martin Shaw Woods. I wanted to hear the shy bullfinches and catch glimpses of the squirrels. The sweet drops of rain would start to bring nature's magic seasonal change to life as we prepared to return to school. The pathways of Martin Shaw Woods would strengthen from a dusty brown to deep mahogany, reviving a healthy glow I always loved to see return. I thought about how much I would miss my forest friends.

PART II

OVER AND OVER

CHAPTER 5

True As Can Be

I felt numb for days. I hoped I'd just stay at my biological parents' house for a day or two, play with my sister, and be sent back to Mum and Dad in Ratby. I was still in Leicester, but a different town: New Parks. I couldn't believe that I had just left my foster family and friends, but I thought I would at least be allowed to go to see them one more time before I went to Nigeria.

Fostering today is considered a practice where children are taken from their biological families into a place or home of safety due to reasons such as drug misuse, domestic violence or any other unfortunate situations that might be happening in the birth parents' home.

None of these were the reasons I got fostered, or indeed why my other biological siblings got fostered in separate homes.

In the early 1970s, in the UK, there was what was known as 'private fostering'; some people have also termed it 'Farming' (although I wasn't aware of this term at the time). Large numbers of West African parents, particularly Nigerians, came to the UK to study and work (sometimes more than one job) tirelessly to provide for their family as well as send money back home to their parents; whilst also bringing up their children in the UK. It was the increased level of demands faced by most Nigerian parents that forced many to seek white families to 'foster' their children. This made it convenient because it was like a 'live-in' type of arrangement for the fostered child, as opposed to 'daycare nursery', where the birth parents need to pick up their child at some point in the same day. Picking up their child after work on the same day was, in most cases, not feasible because not only did most mothers do more than one job that meant they didn't finish work until very late at night, many of their husbands studied, worked and shuttled back and forth to Nigeria. Some fathers were not always fully present to share the burden of raising a family in the UK. This was the situation in my case. The mothers were left in the UK to also work, study and look after the children. Most mothers struggled with this arrangement since because they were in a foreign land they had to prove that they could perform effectively at work just like their white counterparts. Our mothers had no extended family support network to look after their children in the UK whilst they went to work.

Thousands of Nigerians sought private foster care so that they could focus on working hard and studying to provide a better living for their family. Whilst there was no question as to who had the parental legal right to the child being fostered (the biological parents), the lack of effective communication and proper formal systems in place at the time meant that the biological family, for all kinds of different reasons, would choose the time they wanted their child back from the fostering family, with little or no notice given. This, of course, resulted in traumatic experiences such as that my foster family and I encountered.

I loved my biological family, and I had a special bond with my little sister. It was fun being with my big brothers and my dad, who doted on me and played with my sister and me, getting us to dance to Nigerian music together. I enjoyed the piggybacks I got from my big brothers. I looked forward to seeing them at the weekends, but I had a routine and was used to always going back to my foster family.

The one complication I experienced, having two sets of parents, was that I mirrored what my foster family did. They addressed my biological parents by their first names, and I did too. Once I was settled (or at least once I'd got used to the idea that this was my new life), it was apparent that I needed to adapt, quick, to never going back to my foster family and never going back to see my friends at school. Life was now only with my biological family. After being told off a few times for calling my biological parents by their first names, I soon made amends. The adjustment was swift.

There was a clear sense that my biological family were not receptive to me talking about my foster family. I wrote several letters to my foster family and friends and gave them to my birth mum; I never got responses back. I always anticipated receiving their messages; I'd ask my birth mum almost every day. I cried nearly every night in private so that no one would notice.

At first I talked to my biological family about my foster family and friends, but I learnt to stop talking about them as they showed little interest. I was not as communicative as I used to be; I was frequently hushed.

Before we left for Nigeria, a home practitioner for foster children visited me. He asked me several questions about going to Nigeria and whether or not I wanted to leave the UK.

My mum had spoken to me the day before. She told me how beautiful Nigeria was. I believed that there would be monkeys swinging from tree to tree. I thought there might also be a need to run inside the house for fear of being eaten up by stray tigers. She said it was full of beautiful exotic fruits. We would have a massive sweet shop, and we would go to many fun places that I'd never seen before. She then said something along the lines of, 'A man will come to see you tomorrow and ask if you want to go to Nigeria. You'll say you want to go, won't you?'

I looked at her and nodded.

'Yes, Mummy. Will I get to see monkeys outside? Can I have one as a pet?'

'Okomi,' she said, 'if you want to see monkeys swinging around, we'll take you to the zoo.'

The only Yoruba word I understood at the time was 'okomi', meaning 'my dear', so I knew she meant something along the lines of 'Nigeria is more developed than that, my dear.'

Despite some of my difficult times in coming to terms with the fact that I would never live with my foster family again, I did have a wonderful time with my biological family. Before we left Leicester, the best times were playing with my sister with our Sindy dolls, and writing made-up stories with drawings to go with them. My sister and I were incredibly close, and we'd go to the fields behind our house and pick daisies to make necklaces, rings and bracelets.

I particularly loved being Daddy's precious girl. As the first daughter after three big brothers, I felt like Dad's favourite. I was 'Daddy's little princess'. I remember him telling me that as a toddler. He'd play with me and we had our favourite game, where he would pretend to steal my nose. He'd place his thumb in between his two fingers, saying, 'Look, Basirat, I've got your nose.' I would cry, climb on his belly and tug at his nose, trying to pull it off and put it on mine. He'd be laughing so hard, thinking, no doubt, what a daft little two- or three-year-old I was. In anguish from me pulling his nose, he'd plead with me, shouting, 'Touch your nose, touch your nose, it's still there.' I would feel my nose, laugh so much, and he'd give me a piggyback.

Our mum worked in the textile department in Lewis' Department Store in Leicester. She would buy gorgeous and exquisite print material and take my sister and me to her seamstress. We'd be measured and have the seamstress sew pretty matching clothes for us.

When my sister and I went out with our mum, people – particularly older men and women – would stop us and compliment our pretty dresses. They would ask us all the time if we were twins. I remember almost always jumping in to say, 'No, we're not twins. I'm older.'

The first time I remember having any type of physical pain was when I started to have the occasional earache after moving in with my biological family. It intensified at night, so my mum decided to take me to see the doctor. There was no real explanation for it. I remember my mum putting drops of oil in my ear before I went to bed. I often went to her in the middle of the night, complaining that it was hurting a lot. I stopped eating as I used to. My mum always forced me to eat at the table, and I got told off regularly for eating too slowly. My dad would tell my mum that I was losing a lot of weight.

CHAPTER 6

A New Beginning

My biological family and I travelled to Nigeria, as planned, in October 1980. I was eight years old. It felt like we were on the ship for a lifetime. It was quite a nice trip with my family; it was lovely to go on the deck to see the endless sea and sky at night.My sister and I wore brand-new matching clothes every day with matching headbands.

We got to Nigeria about fifteen days after we boarded the ship. The environment was different; a continuous envelope of heat, and the dusty smell of the air was constant. It took a while to get used to it. It suddenly brought home to me the realisation that I was very far away from my foster family. I remember tears frequently rolling down my cheeks unexpectedly.

Being with my birth siblings, my mum and my dad made settling into Nigeria a little easier. We all had each other, even though it was in an unfamiliar environment. It was burning hot, like nothing I had ever been used to before, even when we went to Torquay in the summer. It was humid, scorching hot. I remember thinking we were always walking on the road, but it was because there were no clear demarcations between the pavement and the road. The passing cars would drive by, leaving behind a trail of dust in the previously stagnant air. The dusty particles reflected the sun-rays, taking on the appearance of a plume of smoke. The stale smell of the air was suffocating.

The one thing that stood out was the language that I heard people speak out loud in the streets. I didn't understand what people were saying. Our mum and dad were brilliant at teaching us the different way of life though. They would invite their brothers, sisters and aunties to meet us, and they would teach us how to speak Yoruba – the language spoken in the south-western part of Nigeria. We were in Lagos state. At the time, Lagos was the capital of Nigeria. Abuja replaced it in 1991.

We all struggled with the heat. In the first few days after our arrival, there were times when there would be a sudden power cut. It was quite scary when this happened at night. My sister and I would shout as our brothers crept up and scared us. The power cuts were quite frustrating, and I would go to my mum, asking why the lights always got turned off. She said it was a usual thing that happened in Nigeria.

We heard constant echoes of people shouting from outside when there was a power cut. At first I couldn't get my head around it, but it soon became the norm for me too. When the power got reinstated, people from outside or neighbouring homes would shout, 'NEPA ti mu na dey O.' My siblings and I later joined in on this mini celebration of restored power. Our mum or dad would say, 'Kids, put the fans on. NEPA has brought back the light.'

I frequently noticed how most people added exclamatory words 'O' after a sentence. My sister and I would giggle when we heard people use this connotation. It was used to denote more than one reaction. It was used to answer a call, used in agreement and it was also used to reiterate a point.

NEPA stands for National Electric Power Authority. It used to be the organisation that governed the use of electricity in Nigeria. The Power Holding Company of Nigeria (PHC or PHCN) took over in 1999.

Our mum and dad were Muslims. We all had to go to the mosque regularly. We were all supposed to fast during Ramadan and were encouraged to first fast half-days before easing into the full day. Although we would sometimes forget and eat throughout the day, particularly my sister and I, we would still wake up to eat the 'pre-dawn meal', suhoor, known as sãrì in Yoruba. It was great fun eating at dawn.

We learnt how to cook delicious meals. My siblings and I would regularly take turns to stand in the kitchen to watch our mum cook the most wonderful traditional meals.

There was a sweet shop next door owned by our neighbours. The first time we were made aware of it, my sister and I were excited and dashed off to buy our favourite sweets. I asked for a dib dab sherbet sweet and a Marathon chocolate bar. The people in the shop laughed at me and said, 'Shaarbat ko, Shakirat ni.' *You won't get sherbet. You'll get something else.*

The shopkeeper mocked the fact that we asked for British sweets in a little shop. They handed over coconut candy instead. It was sweet and prepared by frying grated coconut mixed in sugar. We liked it.

We would also buy a type of candy called *ekona Gowon,* which meant 'Gowon's finger'. It was named after Yakubu Gowon, the Head of State of Nigeria between1966 and 1975. The history of this sweet is unknown, but it appeared to have been popular after the Gowon/Ojukwu Biafran war. The sweet was long and got narrower as you licked it. To me at the time, it was more like a tactical knife, made with both smooth and serrated blade, coated with hardened sugar. The *ekona Gowon* sweet got so sharp at the sides and tip that my tongue would often bleed as I sucked on it. I soon got used to crunching it all up before it sliced my tongue up.

We got to know our grandparents on both our mum and dad's side, but it was mostly our maternal grandmum that often came to stay with us.

My sister and I giggled as we were held tight by our grandmum.

Mum said, 'Girls, Grandmum is saying, "My children. My very own children welcome home. Children from the UK."'

My sister and I giggled again as we struggled to get out of the entanglement of our grandmum's arms.

She came over regularly to look after us when our mum went to work. She'd bring a lot of local indigenous food from our hometown in Oyo state, things like *eko tutu*. She'd give this to me, and I'd spit it out as quickly as I put it in my mouth. I'd look over to my mum and say, 'Mum, what's that?'

'Eat it up, Basirat. You never like eating anything,' my mum would say. 'It's made from maize and hardened by heating constantly on a stove, just like custard. But this is more natural without the yellow colouring. Once it's cooled down, it gets wrapped in the leaves to keep it fresh.'

'I prefer coloured custard,' I'd mumble under my breath.

Our grandmum also brought a few snacks like *awin*. The first time Grandmum gave me this 'sweet', I popped it in my mouth, and it felt velvety and rusty. Mum looked at me and said, 'No, you don't eat all of it.'

I spat it out. Mum took one of the sweets and peeled off the black coating. She said it was an African fruit. She explained further, saying that the leaf extract of the fruit was popularly used as a herbal concoction to help cure malaria.

Our grandmum was fun, loving and very neat. She would wake up very early, sweep the whole house and place a few balls of camphor between our clothes and our sheets in the wardrobes. We would usually be woken up by the strong smell of hot herbal concoctions. Our grandmum put different types of thin sticks, leaves, bark and roots in a pot and boiled them all up, infusing them in boiling water. She gave us two different types of these herbal drinks. Most times, she forced us to drink them. I felt like I was going to pass out! I'd stay behind my brothers, pushing them to go first. The drinks were no Babycham shandy that I used to plead to have back in Leicester. The mixture didn't taste like my lovely Pop cherryade either. They were as bitter as hell! Our mum explained that *agbo jedi-jedi* cured any ailments that resulted in backaches or abdominal pains from eating too many sweets, while *agbo iba* helped prevent us from getting malaria.

Our grandmum loved to dance with us. She'd hold our hands and sing songs in our native language. With her hands spread out and looking straight at me, she'd slightly bend to make more deliberate emphasis on the wordings. The first few times she sang, I didn't understand a word. As she danced, Mum repeated after her to teach me the interpretation:

'Ni to ri Arike omo mi, ni mo se'n wa o, mi o wa lasan.'

'Ni to ri Arike omo mi ni mo shen jo o, mi o jo lasan.'

My mum said, 'You see, *she comes because of you Arike, she doesn't come for the sake of coming.*' and '*She's dancing because of you too.*'

'Am I Arike, Mum?' I asked.

'Yes, that's your Oriki,' my mum replied. 'It's your cultural attribute given to you. It's a form of praise poetry in Yoruba. Your name, Arike, means "black beauty that shows love and care towards others and takes people's feelings into consideration". Orikis are the names to praise a child for the pride they bring to the family, or to describe an expected character trait that the family believes a child was born with.'

With keen interest, I replied, 'That's nice.'

Although I had fun and blended in with my siblings during the day, I rarely slept at night. I woke up quite a lot at nights in the first few months after arriving in Nigeria. I'd go to my mum and shake her with vigour, asking her to take me back to my foster family in Leicester.

Besides putting aside my sadness at not seeing my foster family, I also had to deal with switching from using my left hand to my right hand. I was left-handed before I came to Nigeria, but due to the negative cultural connotations of the left hand, I had to stop writing and eating with it. In Nigeria there is a general belief that the left hand is for dirty things, like cleaning yourself when you go to the toilet. Whenever I forgot to use my right hand, I'd get my hand slapped. I got a smacked wrist from just about anyone. It could be the shopkeeper when I went to buy sweets next door and handed him or her 20 kobos for a candy. I could get slapped on the wrist by aunties or uncles. I would have my pencil snatched out of my left hand whenever I forgot to use my right hand. I struggled to write with my right hand initially, and I would get frustrated that my handwriting was no longer as neat as it was when I was left-handed.

It took some time before I fully grasped the rapid changes that were occurring, in terms of starting a new school, learning the traditional language of Yoruba, and the whole environment that was very different from the UK.

It wasn't too brutal. After all, my siblings and I had each other's back, although it was annoying when I got placed two classes below where I should have been because I couldn't understand or speak the language, Yoruba. Even though I faced different struggles, I excelled at school from the first year of getting to Nigeria. I had always enjoyed studying and loved the rewards of my high performance as a child. My dad was very proud because I was intelligent.

My world, as an eight-year-old, felt split in two. During the day, I focused on my studies and got involved in family activities. I played with my dolls too. At night I reverted to another me. I cried in bed because I was missing my foster family and was very upset that I hadn't received any letters from them. I didn't receive any from my best friend either, although I wrote several letters. There was so much going on that I was on auto-pilot during the day, and at night when I was lonely, I'd reflect and think about Ratby.

I attended a junior school at the time called Ewe-Nla [Big leaf] Primary School Crescent. My school was an evergreen field with children in a white and green uniform. It gave it a kind of freshness that made you feel welcome. I made a lot of friends, told them all about my best friend Kerry, and attempted to talk about my white mum and dad, but they just didn't understand, so I stopped talking about them to my classmates.

Although I eventually settled down, I had to contend with the fact that I had a strong Leicester accent. Kids at school made fun of my accent. A particular boy called Chibuzo would shout from afar, 'Bashiiiiraaa. What'ya doing?' At first, he was quite annoying, but we later became good friends and often walked home from school together.

My class teachers were quite fond of me. I was the assistant class monitor, and I was usually the listening ear to my friends. Some of my friends called me 'mother-hen'. The one thing I was guilty of in school was not having enough noise maker names on the list that I wrote in the absence of the class monitor. He carried out more 'important' tasks, like helping to mark test scripts. Boys were the heads of the class. Girls were the assistants, regardless of academic attainment. I considered this to be unfair, as there were times I knew I performed better than the class monitor. I had a cane to hold. Students didn't get scared when they saw me holding the long stick. They knew I didn't feel comfortable having it. I never really got used to holding the cane. It seemed strange.

In the playground, the games were very different from the ones I was used to in Ratby, but I would watch and see how my classmates played them, and I'd join in. The most popular game that we played was called Ten-Ten. I wasn't as quick as some of my friends to start with, but soon became a pro. We would play this in the rain; we'd clap our hands vigorously in a fast rhythm, while swinging our foot forward in alternate and contrasting movements. I'd often try to teach them the games I played in Ratby Primary. The one game they particularly enjoyed was 'A sailor went to sea, sea, sea'.

I quickly had a best friend, Bolanle. I took a liking to her because she had also come back from the UK and had a British accent. I always made a point of telling her about my other best friend, Kerry. I thought I would be betraying Kerry if I didn't.

I'd also keep Bolanle sweet. We enjoyed each other's company, and we'd swap food at dinner times. We liked playing together, and she'd tell me about her life in the UK. Our friendship came to an abrupt end two years later when my class teacher told me that she had left school. I was distraught.

Another close friend I had was Toluwalase. He was very calm and we often played at break time when I wasn't with my other girl friends.

When I got upset from missing my foster family, he would keep me company and make me laugh, distracting me, temporarily.

I'd regularly chat with the dinner lady. She was very nice. I always helped the teachers with books, and I'd take them to the school office. There were a lot of Ghanaian teachers in my school. I performed exceptionally well in the Maths and English lessons that they taught. Their accents sounded friendly.

I began to thrive academically. I was studious and scooped up a lot of prizes in various subjects. I had a double promotion when I was in Year 4 (third grade). My parents objected to it as they said it would take me to the final year in primary school. They said I should go through all the classes so I would not miss out on essential topics.

I would regularly get a special prize from my dad for topping the class. He awarded children in the family who came first in their class with a 'Cross' pen (similar to a Parker pen). I scooped up all the Cross pens every term in the first year of living in Nigeria. It was remarkable to be rewarded with pens because we used pencils in school.

It was reassuring, knowing I was unique to my dad. Although I missed my foster family back in the UK, I loved being with my biological family. My dad reinforced and emphasised, through the rewards I received, that my efforts at school were not going unnoticed.

The noticeable difference between the UK and Nigeria was the cultural difference in attributing a high level of respect in Nigeria to those older than you. I recall our aunties being horrified when they heard me call my older brothers by their names. Our aunties would yell at us, saying, 'Basirat Shey wan shey'egbeeh ni?'

'Don't call them by their names O,' another auntie would say, in a strong Yoruba accent. 'He's not your mate, Basirat, so you have to call him Brother Olu.'

I'd often hear the phrase: 'Is he your mate?' or 'Is she your mate?' and not understand why mate was added at the end. This, I'd be told, means someone is not the same age as you, and, for that reason, you have to show them respect. I was gradually getting used to the slang and different phrases used in Nigeria.

I often tried to get around the 'respectful' way of addressing my brothers. I'd walk up to my brothers and tap them on the shoulder instead of calling out their names. That didn't last though, and my dad ensured that I learnt to kneel when greeting anyone older than me (apart from my brothers).

CHAPTER 7

Ending A Beginning

My sister and I were like two peas in a pod. We went everywhere together, even to the sweet shop that was just next door to us. That day, however, would be different. It had been a year since we'd moved to Nigeria.

My mum came up to me. She tapped me gently and said, 'Go and get dressed; we are going out.'

I was about to run to get my sister, but my mum stopped me, saying, 'No need to call her, she's not coming.'

Going out with my mum without my sister felt extremely strange. I asked her why my sister wasn't coming along, but she said, 'Don't worry; you're the only one going.'

I knew better than to ask any further questions.

My mum and I travelled for about an hour. As a nine-year-old, I remember it feeling like forever. The sun was blazing and it was noisy. I asked her why the man hanging onto the side of the bus always shouted. She said he was a bus conductor, and he was announcing what direction the bus was going in. I asked her where we were going, and she said to see someone. I was tempted to ask who, but said nothing. I remember missing my sister, thinking how far along we would have got with our story writing or playing with our Sindy dolls by now.

We finally got to our destination. I was immediately blown away by the colossal house. The gates were tall and painted in light blue and white. They matched the house a few yards back from the beautiful gate. It stood out from the few buildings around it. Pink and red roses were overhanging the fence.

My mum rang the bell, and a man ran towards us. He had lovely jet-black hair and a beaming smile on his face. He immediately ran towards me, barely saying hello to my mum. He picked me up and said, 'She's got my eyes and nose.'

I was quite confused by all that was happening. I didn't know why this man was excited while I was expressionless. While I was still in the air, I looked over to my mum, and she said, 'That's your dad.'

With my eyes still fixed on her and away from the man who was putting me down, I said, 'Dad is at home.'

I said nothing else. I was speechless and felt like I might have misheard what my mum had just said. Did she just say the man that I don't know is my father? Did she say he was my daddy?

She did say the man was my father.

We proceeded to go inside the house. He took us up to his room. On the wall was a big picture of me. Still in shock from the whole confusing scenario of just being introduced to a man who was now my real dad out of nowhere, I said nothing. I remember being fussed over by two women. He introduced me to them and said they were my stepmothers.

We were taken downstairs to the dining table. There were different types of food dishes. There were a variety of fizzy drinks, commonly referred to as 'minerals' in Nigeria. I barely touched my meal. The man asked my mum about my eating habits. He said I was a little on the thin side. My mum told me to eat up and mentioned my poor eating habits, saying it had got worse since our arrival in the country. She said I never liked eating. She said I was a very sluggish eater even when I did decide to have some food. He asked her how I was doing in school. She said I was doing exceedingly well and that I always topped my class. My mum looked at me and smiled, saying, 'I'm quite proud of her in that respect.'

Throughout the conversation, I was looking down at my plate, still filled with rice and meat. To put it mildly, I had a lot on my plate – physically and metaphorically.

I gazed at both my mum and him, feeling confused and uncertain about what they were telling me about family dynamics. As they continued chatting, I saw two cute toddler boys smiling at me. I shifted the food back and forth on my plate. My mum was at this moment engrossed in a conversation with him when I politely said, 'Excuse me please, may I leave the table?'

He looked at me, a big smile on his face, possibly impressed with my good manners, and said, 'You've hardly touched your food. OK, OK, go on. I see you want to play with your brothers.'

I left the table and went to the sitting room with the two gorgeous little boys. Both of them were two years old. I watched them as I thought to myself, *Are they now my brothers?* I watched both of them play together, but I hardly got involved. My mind wandered back and forth. I was thinking of how I would tell my sister and brothers back home.

We left to go home, and I remember barely uttering a word on the way back. I just couldn't quite process everything. A thought suddenly jumped into my head. My eyes welled with tears. Tapping my mum gently on her arm, I said, 'Mum, does that mean my sister is not my real sister anymore?'

She looked at me and said, 'She is still your real sister. She's your half-sister. You have the same mum, but you have a different dad to your sister and brothers.'

I looked away and stared out of the window, tears rolling down my cheeks for the rest of the journey back home.

My beginning was ending. I remember thinking how badly I wanted to go back to my foster parents in Leicester. I felt different and, all of a sudden, alone.

PART III

LIFE PROMISES LIFE

CHAPTER 8

Changing Times

Nothing could have prepared me for the magnitude of discovering this news as a nine-year-old. I immediately shut down. I felt my world crashing down again; it was tough for me to make sense of the rapid and drastic changes.

The effect of knowing that my siblings were no longer my full birth siblings was hurtful. I remember getting back home on the day I saw my real dad and not uttering a word. I felt numb and different. I thought if I didn't tell my siblings I now had another dad to them, they'd never find out, and I could pretend that I was still their full birth sister. I felt I had lost control of my life.

The different thoughts racing through my head were debilitating. I felt weak, knowing that I was no longer my loving and adorable dad's little girl. I'd grown closer to him after leaving my foster parents, but now our relationship felt threatened. I couldn't easily come to terms with the fact that my 'real dad' was now my stepdad.

I felt dazed a lot of the time. I had loads of 'poor me' moments, and it was quite difficult for me to come to terms with the fact that I was the only one, out of the five of us, who had a different father. It hurt deeply, and I started, from the moment I was introduced to my father, beginning to feel that my siblings were 'one', and I was another. I'd think about all the good times I had in Leicester, and the short time I'd spent with them all as one big happy family. I would start to think about how I would cope without my siblings if I had to move in with my birth father. I was growing up fast, having thoughts that made me fretful.

I asked my mum if I would ever go away from her and my siblings. She would look at me and say, 'Not yet, Basirat.'

I would continue to ask, 'But would I ever leave you and go on my own?'

She would say I didn't need to start worrying about that now.

People often said that I was slow and dragged my heels. I started to get used to it. I'd be walking with an aunt, and she'd shout and say, 'Basirat, hurry up! Your mum did say you were very slow.'

Our grandmum also said that it took me too long to sweep a small area, compared to how long it took my little sister to carry out the same task. I do recall not being incredibly graceful in my movements. I remember an uncle also saying that I was slow in carrying out tasks that required little or no time to finish.

Playing with my sister had been one of my most enjoyable and most precious fun times before I knew my real dad. After meeting him, I would often gaze at her as we played with our Sindy dolls. As she had her head down, moving the toy to make it walk, one leg at a time as we often did, I'd be far away, absent-minded, thinking that I no longer had her as a 'real sister'. The thought shattered me.

I don't remember ever having a discussion with my siblings about the sudden change, and I didn't want to either; I felt that I was no longer fully part of the family. This feeling, of course, was not reciprocated as far as I knew; it was just how I felt. I became overly sensitive or sometimes paranoid. If my siblings were all together without me for one reason or the other, I'd tearfully go to them and say, 'Why didn't you call me?'

The intensity of my earaches returned when I was around nine. I woke up almost every other night, my head tipped to one side in agony and I'd be wailing in excruciating pain. The earache I'd had before we came to Nigeria had come back, only this time about ten times worse!

My mum would put a bit of oil in my ear to help me go back to sleep. The pain would persist, but I'd fall asleep, waking up with my pillow soaked in tears.

When I went to wake my mum up, she would get upset with me. She often had to wake up early to go to work. She'd say I always had something wrong with me. My siblings also noticed I was always the one saying something was hurting me somewhere.

I was once playing outside with a cousin, and I had a sudden earache. I dropped to the ground in pain. She sighed and said, 'Omo aje butter ni eh jo!'

'I'm not a spoilt child or a weakling!' I shouted back.

She went on to say that it must be the fact that I'd stayed with a white family that spoilt me, and that had resulted in me being so different from my siblings. She said none of the others had so many physical ailments, so it must be that I was spoilt and could not cope with the Nigerian way of living.

I stopped going to my mum in the middle of the night when the earache intensified. I would cry in bed and stay awake for most of it.

My mum had a lot on her plate, settling in Nigeria. She was an independent woman and she needed to stay driven. She had just been offered a secretarial role at the Federal Radio Corporation of Nigeria. Working at FRCN was a demanding job that required her to start early and often come back home late in the evening.

From the age of ten, I had a big distraction from always missing my foster family. I was responsible for looking after our baby brother. He was born a few months after my tenth birthday. I had the responsibility of taking him to his childminder every morning before I went to school. I also picked him up as soon as I got back from school. I adored my baby brother and would tie him on my back with a wrapper (a piece of fabric tied around the waist) and use another one just around his bum to keep him from sliding down my back. I struggled to secure the long cloth around my baby brother, and I would continuously use both my hands to support him from falling. Everyone used to call me his 'little mum'. Before our mum got back from work, I'd make sure he was clean by changing his nappies. I often hurt myself with the big nappy pins that I used on both sides of his terry towelling nappies because I'd place my finger so close to the pin, preventing it from pricking my baby brother. It was fun making his bottled milk. I took pride in making sure he was happy and well fed. I would give him one Farley's Rusk biscuit, and I'd eat one too.

Although I stopped going to my mum for the pain of the tinnitus that persisted, I went to wake her up when I started having nightmares. I would wake up, almost every other night, in a sweat; I'd see black clustered holes that made me scream. I'd feel very ill, and I'd go to her, explaining what I was seeing and that when I closed my eyes during the day, I would often see big black lumps or very tiny ones that scared me. When I was shown anything with clustered holes, I would get very agitated and uneasy.

Another change at home was that it was no longer mandatory for me to go to the mosque. When my stepdad and siblings all went, my mum would say I could go if I wanted to.

I didn't feel like part of the family any more. I'd never really liked going to the mosque, because I wanted to play, but it was different now. My siblings were obliged to go, and I felt left out. It hurt that I had a choice. I didn't want an option. I just wanted to do what my siblings had to do.

My birth dad was a Christian, and that automatically meant I was too. I didn't get forced to partake in Muslim activities. I felt crushed and ashamed that I was different, and I started to withdraw from my stepdad because I felt guilty that I was no longer his daughter. Although he rarely reprimanded me, because I was generally well behaved and obedient, I always thought he'd stopped telling me off altogether. I was getting to be overly sensitive about anything. I wanted him to tell me off sometimes so that I could feel that things hadn't changed. My feelings were that the family dynamics had changed, because of me, for ever.

Above: Me and my baby brother on his first birthday.

He'd still play with me, and never said I wasn't his daughter. But I withdrew over time, even though I desperately wanted more reassurance. My going back and forth at the weekends to stay with my birth father made it difficult to stay fully connected to my stepdad. Sometimes I cried in exhaustion. I wanted to go back to Leicester and be with my foster parents even more. I yearned for letters from them. I would write letters, telling them that the dad they thought was my dad was no longer my dad. I would give my mum more messages, but had no letters back. I felt neglected. I needed reassurance that my foster parents still cared for me, but not having letters from them made me deeply sad. I clung on to the good times I'd spent with them and would often talk about them to anyone who listened.

CHAPTER 9

Dancing Through It All

At nine years old my life started all over again. I now had a new dad. My mum managed the transition to my real dad the best she could. I started by going to visit him, my half-siblings and their mums at the weekends. At twelve years old, I eventually moved in with my new family.

I'd give anything just to be held in the arms of my foster mum right now, I thought to myself. *I just really need her soft, warm, tender arms wrapped around me.* I'd often close my eyes and feel her tenderness.

On the day I left to go to my biological father, there were no tears. It felt rushed, and there was no time for ceremonious departures. I hugged my siblings, mum and stepdad before rushing off to my dad's driver. He was known as Baba Ramo – it's common for parents to be called Baba or Mama, followed by the name of their firstborn child. It was as if I was going on a day's outing. I didn't feel one way or the other.

I got in the well air-conditioned white Toyota Cressida. It was clean and smelt fresh. Baba Ramo proceeded to drive away as I waved to my family. I sat in the front next to him. He quickly started to crack jokes. He asked me a lot of questions about the UK. I was warming up to him and liked that he was interested in what was important to me. I found him to be very friendly and funny. He joked about how I would carry out lots of chores, like carrying heavy wood used to make fires, to prepare the food. He said I'd have big basins of vegetables on my head when we travelled to the village.

I quickly said, 'I thought they were nice people when I went to visit them last time.'

With a big grin on his face, he said, 'Oh no, that was because it was your first time. They were trying to get you all settled down first.'

He noticed how quiet I was and took a quick side glance at me. He laughed and said, 'I'm joking. You won't do all that.'

With a giggle, I looked at him and said, 'You are funny.'

Baba Ramo had just pulled up to the driveway of the house, and it suddenly dawned on me that I had left my sister and family and would no longer live with them. At my dad's house, everyone hugged me and helped me get my things out of the car. The house had a vast compound with a back garden beautifully surrounded by fruits such as papaya, coconut and banana trees.

Toyin, short for Oluwatoyin, was now my name. As a Christian, my dad had signed an affidavit to change my name, removing my Muslim names, and changing my surname to Balogun.

I had my own room. I thought it was cool to have a place to myself and only have to share it with my aunties when they came over for weekend visits. There were always a lot of people in the house. We had uncles and aunties from my dad's village who would visit and have a sleepover for a few nights. They sometimes came over for weeks or even months at a time. I enjoyed their company.

My dad had relatives from the village who maintained the house and washed his clothes. He also had two drivers. He had one for him, and the other one was for the kids and my stepmums. Other workers came to the house to carry out other minor repairs and gardening duties. He took pride in the maintenance of the house and the surroundings. The house would get thoroughly fumigated once a month to get rid of rodents, pests, and any other insects in the home. We would all vacate the house for around three to four hours until all the fumes had fully evaporated and it was safe to return.

My dad worked as a Personnel Director for a major glass company in Lagos and ran two businesses of his own – a bakery within the compound of the house and a distributorship of Guinness and other alcoholic beverages for retailers in neighbouring towns. The building unit for the distribution was just a few yards outside of the house. He was a knowledgeable man and would often tell us all how he always topped his class in both his junior and high school days and would say how well he excelled in university. All my friends' dads had come first in their classes too; I always wondered which fathers came second.

He was very charming, generous, outspoken and well respected in the community. He was also highly placed at work and spoke impeccable English. He had studied in the UK and lived there for some time. He was regularly invited to universities and other academic events to be the keynote speaker on various business and personnel administration matters. He was financially comfortable and provided us all with everything we needed. We all listened to him tell us stories of how hard he had to work to make sure his parents and siblings lacked nothing.

Although I was close with my half-siblings, it took me a long time to bond with my dad. I just didn't or couldn't come to terms with the fact that I now had a new dad, and I was a little withdrawn. I felt betrayed by my mum but was grateful that she had made sure that I had been visiting him every weekend from the age of nine. Seeing him and his family regularly before I finally moved in made the transition as smooth as it could be. His upbeat personality made it slightly more comfortable for me to get into conversations with him, but it still took about three years to accept that he was indeed my real, birth father.

By the time I'd moved in just before my twelfth birthday in August 1984, although I was very reserved and quiet, I did start to get into conversations with my stepmums. I helped out with chores and also played with my half-siblings. I bathed them regularly and dressed them up. Some of them were toddlers and babies when I arrived. Bonding with my 'new' half-brothers and sisters came naturally. They loved and bonded with me in equal measure. But there were times I felt socially disoriented and I missed my half-sister most of all.

My dad tried to make me as comfortable as he thought fit. He'd buy anything I needed. He would ask one of my aunts to take me shopping. She took me out to buy clothes, shoes and just about anything I wanted.

I'd often hope my dad would ask how I was coping without my foster parents and how things had been in the years he wasn't present. I thought that he had probably asked my mum everything he needed to know. He was particularly interested in learning how well I was performing academically in primary school.

With a lot of children in the house, it was almost always going to be impossible for him to pay any attention to how bumpy my life experiences had been and how the adverse childhood experiences had affected me so far. Due to the busyness and various activities that went on, there were times I just got on with my new life and that helped me cope a little bit better. Although I missed my stepdad, mum, brothers and, most especially, my sister, I was now enjoying the abundance of food and other luxuries that my dad's wealth afforded.

I was happy that I no longer had to eat food I didn't particularly like. When I'd lived with my mum and my other family, we would often have *ogi* (corn flour) with *akara* (a dish made from peeled beans formed into a ball and then deep-fried in palm or vegetable oil). I didn't like that at all.

At my dad's, I now enjoyed the crunchy Kellogg's Cornflakes and milk that gave me a sense that I was closer to Ratby in Leicester. We would make some of our food from scratch. Learning how to prepare traditional foods was fun. I learnt how to make some of the traditional foods like *garri* from cassava tubers. My siblings and I used a mesh and tossed the grated cassava. We sieved the grains and subsequently roasted them in a big hot circular hollow tray. Once we finished the process of turning the cassava tubers into *garri,* we made *eba,* a traditional meal usually served with a delicious bowl of *egusi* (blended melon seeds) stew with fish or meat. I loved making it more than I loved eating it.

Going to church was a big part of the routine. We all went every Sunday without fail. My dad was a warden in the Anglican church that we attended. It was less than two miles from our house. We were a very well-known family by most, if not all, the church members.

We had prayer nights, at 8 pm, daily. There was a bell that we rang just before 8 pm to get everyone seated in the sitting room. We would start by having what was called a 'praise and worship'. This was an initial session of singing and thanking God that lasted about five to ten minutes. The prayer session usually lasted about thirty to forty-five minutes.

Christmas celebrations were special events, and my stepmums and aunties from our village would spend days before Christmas and on Christmas Day cooking different types of meals. On Christmas Day, there would be a whole lot of beef and chicken dishes and fried rice or jollof rice with a mixture of fizzy drinks, beers and a variety of fine wines and champagnes. We had a lot of big celebrations. At Christmas time or naming ceremonies (which seemed to happen once a month), chairs and canopies got hired. Workers would set them all up and we would party all night long.

As my siblings grew up, they would accompany me and the house helps to take food to all the surrounding neighbours on Christmas Day. It would generally be distributed to those who were less fortunate and to Muslims who were not celebrating Christmas. The Muslims around us usually reciprocated during their festive seasons too.

Sometimes we'd go to our grandparents in the village in Ogun state. My granddad was kind and gentle. He had a great sense of understanding others and would often sit us all down and tell us fascinating tales about when he was a child.

We'd often go to the stream to fetch buckets of water. We didn't have to, but I loved experiencing village life. We'd go with kids that were around five or six years old. They'd balance the buckets nicely on their heads. They folded up a long cloth and helped me place my bucket on my head. They'd have their buckets full of water when we got back home, and mine would probably only fill a tablespoon, due to the instability of the bucket on my head. It swayed back and forth, tipping out most of the water. But it was fun to go to the streams, seeing the fresh, free-flowing ice cold water.

During the Easter breaks, we went to a place called Whispering Palms Beach Resort in Badagry, Lagos, with our extended family members. It was around twenty-six miles from where we lived. It had tall palm trees and fresh, beautiful greenery with a clean beach area where we had picnics.

Our birthdays were other special occasions we celebrated. Since there were a lot of us, it seemed like we had one birthday every month of the year. Our dad would go all out on having big birthday parties for each one of us, particularly when we reached significant milestones. We invited our friends, cousins, people from our church and neighbours.

Due to a lot of forthcoming school entrance exams, my dad got a private tutor for me so that I could prepare extensively to go to secondary school. He had very high expectations of me and didn't have to utter the words to say so.

It was May of the year 1985, I was twelve years old, and the results for secondary school entrance exams were published. I got my Common Entrance Exam results and gained admission into a school called Mayflower Secondary School. It was a secular boarding school run by Dr Tai Solarin, a Nigerian educator, humanist and civil rights pioneer, who was married to Sheila Mary Tuer, a British educator. Queen Elizabeth II awarded Tuer an MBE on 17 October 2007 for her educational services in Nigeria.

Although my dad didn't tell me all the information mentioned above about Mayflower School, he did say that Dr Solarin's wife was a white lady from the UK. My eyes lit up as if he had just said he'd be flying me back to the UK. I did have a few butterflies in my tummy because of the unknown environment of a boarding school. I also had a thought – *I visit my mum, stepdad and siblings now and again at the weekend – what would happen if I was at boarding school?* I was also looking forward to the adventure of being away from home.

Dad said that students at Mayflower school baked their own bread. The school seemed like one that I'd love with all my heart; I felt like it would be similar to schools in the UK. I was very excited and told him how I couldn't wait to start school.

A week later, my dad called me and said he had more exciting news. He had been given a letter of acceptance into a different school – Command Secondary School, Jos. Jos is the capital of Plateau State in the northern part of Nigeria. He said we would be travelling by air since it was over 400 miles away. Although I felt proud that I'd gained admission into another place, I was puzzled, wondering why I needed to know all the information. He knew I was over the moon with Mayflower School, mainly because it had a slight UK attachment to it. I thought to myself, *I'm sure this was obvious to him, and I hope he won't go on about this new school.* I already had images of strict, militant ways at Command School and couldn't bear to think of being flogged, as I'd often heard happened at military schools.

My dad noticed my confused look. Quickly, with a persuasive smile on his face, he began to tell me all the reasons why I would now be attending this other school.

'Toyin, Command Secondary School is a boarding school too. It's in Jos and is a military school, a very prestigious one. Nigeria is run by the military government and no longer by civilians. This means that if anything goes wrong in the country, such as people protesting against different viewpoints, your school won't be affected.'

None of the military versus civilian conversation made sense to me; I didn't want to understand.

With tears in my eyes, I said, 'I want to go to Mayflower School.'

He said nothing else. I knew this to mean he had made up his mind, and his decision was final. I said nothing and watched as he tidied up the letters on his table. I turned to leave his room.

'Going to a military school will serve you well,' he said. 'You will become sharper and not be as slow anymore.'

His ploy worked, negatively. All I could think of was how I'd have the 'slow coach' behaviour beaten out of me.

'You'll be sham-sham,' he said. This is a term often used by Yorubas to mean quicker and smarter in carrying out tasks.

As I left his room, I felt deflated. I knew I had no further say in the matter. I already spent most of my time writing in my journals; about how I couldn't get rid of the persistent earaches and constant headaches. I'd journal about how desperately I wanted to get in touch with my foster family.

I was getting used to the negative connotation of how slow I was. I rushed to do things to avoid being reprimanded. I made mistakes in the process. I had a lot of 'pity parties' and felt sorry for myself. I'd flood my cheeks with tears for no apparent reason. Just as quickly as I'd burst out crying, I'd wipe my tears as I was interrupted by a sibling, uncle, or an auntie.

CHAPTER 10

Betrayal

I did go to Command Secondary School in Jos, as my dad had decided. I simply had no choice in the decision-making, and it became clear why I had to attend a military school.

It was February 1989, and it was the Harmattan season in Jos. The Harmattan is a season in the West African subcontinent that occurs between the end of November and the middle of March. It is characterised by the dry and dusty north-easterly trade wind, of the same name, which blows from the Sahara Desert over West Africa into the Gulf of Guinea.

When I'd come to Nigeria back in 1980, I'd started school a couple of classes behind because I couldn't grasp the Yoruba language. In 1989 I was seventeen, and in SSS2 (Senior Secondary School 2). This was the equivalent to Year 10 in the UK (ninth grade). I was one of the older kids in my class, as I should have been in Year 12 (eleventh Grade). I often felt embarrassed about being one of the oldest in the class and I'd hope discussions never came up where I had to declare my age.

I was in the science class and had taken up Further Maths as part of my subject choices. Science students were considered to be more intelligent. They had some kind of prestige to them, compared to arts students. The status and reputation attached to being a science student made me feel highly intellectual, even though I was struggling academically, no matter how hard I studied. Reading and writing came naturally to me but I didn't dare to think of being an arts student. There was no way my dad would have allowed it either. Like most Nigerian parents, he had the final say in my subject choices. He wanted me to be a medical doctor, even though I had struggled in science in my Junior Secondary School years.

It was the day of one of our Further Maths tests. I'd practically read through the night for it. I started studying at Night Prep (a study period after supper time, around 6:30 pm to 9 pm) and then carried on into the early hours. We would often go to the classroom area until about 9 pm. When I wasn't with my best friend Fisayo, I'd study with the brainy boys: Tolu, Akinfe, Blaise and Pere. They often taught me Further Maths as we all studied Further Maths. Tolu read all the time. Calling him a bookworm would be an understatement.

Even though I generally studied with them, we were miles apart when it came to achievement, yet I never gave up learning. I never accepted that I wasn't good enough to hang out with the brainy boys. I just had faith in my ability and expected to do well.

We finished studying, and I felt confident. It helped that my classmates had clarified all the tricky areas. I got back to the dormitory and continued to study in a friend's private room after lights out at 10 p.m. She was the head of the dormitory and had the luxury of a place to herself.

The next day, I remember getting dressed early. I dusted on some of my fresh-smelling white talcum powder. I put petroleum jelly on my lips to keep them nice and moist. The stale air was usually harsh and dry on the skin, particularly the lips. I did some more studying and had breakfast in my room so that I didn't have to waste time going to the dining hall. I went straight to the class.

When it was about five minutes until the test, our Further Maths teacher, Mr Oguine, walked in. He was a military officer. He walked with his chest slightly raised and shoulders in a perfect posture. His poise expressed both dignity and grace, and his uniform was always crisp with a well-ironed shirt with sharp shoulder edges.

'Right, please put all your books away,' he said.

I felt confident.

A few minutes later, he said, 'OK, you may start.'

With pen to paper, I took a look at the questions, read through the whole sheet and started racing my pen across the answer sheet. In an instant, my mind went blank. I was suddenly nervous. I raised my head and looked around. Everyone's head was down, their hands were moving furiously on the answer sheet. I could hardly breathe at this point. I felt like I was going to wet myself. I felt the tension in my neck and shoulders. I looked down and started to write things down the best I could remember. I was shaky, almost teary. I kept whispering to myself, 'Toyin, you know these questions! You studied all night for this, and you learnt how to do them. Come on!'

With hardly anything on my answer sheet, after about twenty-five minutes, I heard the Further Maths teacher, in his deep voice, say, 'Five minutes more.' I couldn't believe I'd just heard that. My hands were drenched with sweat. I could hardly grip my pen. I quickly scribbled a few more things down before he said softly but sharply, 'Pens up, please.'

I looked over at the rest of the class. I was hoping that everyone else had struggled with the paper. But most of my friends had smiles on their faces. I got up and handed in my sheet. My friends came over to me from the back of the class.

'That was easier than I expected,' Akinfe said. 'Toyin, you must have been pleased with that. Ah, ah, imagine! Everything we studied last night was what came up.'

With a slight embarrassed look, not wanting to admit that I had just messed up, I very timidly said, 'Yes, I know.'

And I left the classroom.

It would take just two days for the Further Maths teacher to finish marking our scripts. He was an Igbo man (Igbo is the language spoken by those from the eastern part of Nigeria) and he was one of the well-respected teachers. He was very measured in his approach and didn't walk around with a koboko (a long flexible whip made of a cow skin or horsetail) like other teachers did.

Being in a military school, most of our teachers were army officers and would mostly have a *koboko* with them. At times it was used indiscriminately. They could call a student whose shirt was not correctly tucked into his trousers and whip him several times on his bum, causing any slight bit of shirt that was out before he got flogged to fly out completely. The exertion of power sometimes seemed inhumane to me. Sometimes they would have the *koboko* just, in my opinion, to intimidate the students, or at least remind us to be very scared of them. I didn't think we needed reminding, such were their fierce-looking faces, with their crisp, starched military uniforms that made it seem like we were on a battleground.

My Further Maths teacher told me to go to the staff room and wait for him there. It was an open office where all teachers sat to mark test scripts and do all other teaching related tasks. I greeted all of the other teachers in the staff room. They looked at me with a sneaky look that meant, 'Hmm, Toyin is a well-behaved student. I wonder why she is here.'

Students only really went to the school office if they got reprimanded. That time was different. The Further Maths teacher came into the office, asked me to sit down, his desk was not near other teachers' desks so they could hardly hear our conversation. With a puzzled look, he said, 'Toyin, you got zero out of a hundred in your test. Something doesn't quite add up here. I could see that you had studied because there were disjointed workings on the sheet and I really, desperately, wanted to give you a mark but I couldn't. Nothing made sense.'

I remember gazing at him and being very embarrassed by my performance. I felt too ashamed to tell him that I had prepared for the test but that I had been struggling with retaining information.

He looked at me, with such empathy, as if he could read my mind, and asked gently, 'Toyin, is everything OK with you at home?'

No one had ever asked me if I was OK or how I was feeling, not even my parents. I was immediately breathless. I felt Mr Oguine's eyes on me. I thought he could see right through me. My head bowed in shame. I felt shaky, yet numb at the same time.

For the first time, he'd confirmed my thoughts about him. There was something good about our Further Maths teacher. I'd been right all along about Mr Oguine. He wasn't just there to teach you; he was there to care about you. He was interested in issues that affected your wellbeing.

I felt conflicted. I desperately wanted to be probed harder, yet there was a deep pain that ran through my veins. I didn't want him to find out what was going on at home. I felt immeasurable pain at that moment. For the first time, I thought there might indeed be a connection between my performance and the experiences I was going through at home, but I didn't think there should be, because I tried to 'park' my pain to get on with my studies. I'd grown up knowing I was smart and excelled in all subjects. Why should now be any different?

I quickly thought about what answer to give. With a stutter and slow nod, I said, 'E-very-thing is fine, sir.'

He sighed and, with a confused look, shook his head as if to say, 'There is something wrong here, but I won't probe.'

'OK,' he said, 'stay after class tomorrow and I will go through the topic with you one more time.'

I looked to the floor, still embarrassed, and uttered very slowly, 'Thank you, sir,' and walked shamefully out of the staff room.

The question my Further Maths teacher had asked me – 'Is everything OK at home?' – echoed in my head repeatedly. I took a long walk from the dormitory to the class area, even though I'd only just got back from class. I sobbed, feeling rage surge up in me. I was getting angry with my life.

I started to think about how I had always studied hard from the day I started school. I was now frustrated by not performing exceedingly well, which I thought I should because of how hard I studied.

I'd become an average student, sometimes below average in some subjects. I couldn't understand why I'd excelled in primary school and later plummeted into someone scoring zero out of a hundred. Yet I thought it was silly to make excuses for my inadequacies. It never even crossed my mind that it could have anything to do with my experiences so far, particularly my experiences at home.

The more I thought about the question I was asked by my Further Maths teacher, the more I blamed my mum for having me out of wedlock. I was blaming her for sending me off to go live with my real father. I hated my father for what I was thinking about in my head. I was now almost certain that it was because of my experience with him that resulted in my poor performance at school, even though I couldn't prove it.

I got overly worked up as I sat just outside the dining hall, wanting to make sure I had stopped crying before I saw anyone. I didn't want my friends to find out that I had been sobbing uncontrollably.

Another part of me said, 'Toyin, be grateful. You are clothed, you live in a lovely house, and your dad provides you with everything you need. He's placed you in this exclusive public school that many would love to attend.' I had to be happy about all these things.

I was confused about my religious beliefs, too, thinking that something wasn't right there. I didn't understand why I had been put through all of this. I tried to be a good girl, I was respectful, yet I was so unhappy. It weakened my faith.

I'd started to realise that I had unconsciously edited out the nasty bits in my life, but I hadn't known it would get in the way of my studies.

One subject I did excel in was English, especially storytelling. In one class we wrote a story based on the best place we had visited and, needless to say, Torquay in Devon was the place that sprang to mind. I wrote from my heart. When I got my script back, I'd come third in the whole year, out of a total of over 300 students. I was ecstatic!

I'd always felt very expressive when writing. I communicated in a way to overcome the defences I'd built. I allowed people to take a glimpse into my conscience to see me for me, and I was authentic. I felt that I didn't need to hush, so I could pour my heart out! The story allowed me to step outside my brain.

After the scripts were marked, my English teacher said, 'Wow! Toyin, you took me right into your world, O. I am impressed. I felt like I was there with you. You would do exceptionally well as an arts student, O.'

I half smiled at that, thinking, No thank you, I want to be considered smart and intelligent. If only she had pushed me a little harder, maybe, just maybe, as she was a woman, I might have opened up to her.

I was so out of sync with myself that I don't think I would have opened up to her or indeed to anyone, if I'm honest. It was inconceivable that I would let anyone rip apart the stories that I had carefully woven together. I'd edited my experiences carefully. I only ever shared the nice bits to survive and live normally.

Though I did have a lot of study struggles, I had terrific friends. My best friend Fisayo and I did everything together. People often said we were the 'happening chicks'. Although we had split into different classes, we still did most things together when we were in the dormitory. We had great laughs, and when I did talk about my family, I mainly talked about my foster family and how badly I wanted to get in touch with them.

I had two other close friends, Veronica and Uche. As both of them loved reading as much as I did, we often studied together. Some of my friends would comment on how obsessed I was with cleanliness. They noticed I got annoyed if anyone sat on my bed, or if my pillows were out of place. Although I didn't get prizes for the best student, I was often named the neatest girl in the dormitory and, one year, I was named the cleanest girl in the school.

Attending a military boarding school meant harsh discipline in my first few years, particularly the first year. Despite being unwell,

I was once beaten mercilessly by a senior student because I hadn't completed my morning duty. I fainted as a result. It took days for me to recover fully. I'd woken up that morning and felt weak and had a high temperature. My friends took me straight to the school clinic. I was at the clinic for most of the day, lying down on one of two beds in a small room. I got told that I had malaria fever. I was weak and could barely walk. They took me straight to the dormitory to lie down, they went to the dining room to eat and brought some food for me. I couldn't eat, I drank Lucozade instead. It was later that afternoon that I heard the house captain shout,

'Everyone, get outside in the quadrangle, now!'

I remained in bed but was dragged out by the house captain. When my friends saw me being dragged out of bed, they all shouted, 'She's not well!'

The captain ignored them and said, 'Shut up! She'll get flogged ten strokes of the cane because she is unwell, the rest of you will get twenty strokes each.' Apparently our house captain was called out of class during the inspection of the dormitory that morning, by the house mistress (she is responsible for the upkeep of dormitories). It would have been extremely embarrassing for our house captain to be called out of the class. Our dormitory was not clean, so we all got punished for it.

I remember only being told to lie face down and being struck two or three times with the buckled ends of a belt. The next memory I had was when I was on my friend's bed with a hot beverage. My hair was dripping and my clothes were drenched in water. They had poured water on me to get me to wake up after I'd fainted. My friends told me what had happened. They said that the house captain finished striking me the entire ten strokes before realising that I was motionless. It was at that point that she rolled me over with her foot, realising that I had fainted. She was reprimanded by the house mistress and I was allowed to take two weeks off, performing any dormitory chores.

There were times I did enjoy the boarding life. I never wanted to go back home. Although I yearned to eat more nourishing food, I still preferred being with my friends at school. There were only one or two meals that I ate. We had a lot of watery beans that I didn't eat. The only reason I ever wanted to go home was when I thought of how much I missed my half-siblings that I had grown to love.

My friends and I would often sit and chat about our family lives. I was reserved when it came to talking about my family dynamics. I knew all about the family members of my friends, but they hardly knew anything about mine. I avoided talking about my real family in great depth.

The reality was that, no matter how painful it was when I moved from family to family, there were times I did enjoy the diverse and unique characteristics of each family. But I never saw it that way. I was never really made to see it that way. I could never be grateful for the life that I had. The negative aspects of my life overshadowed everything beautiful in my life. I was being eaten up slowly by my insecurities, about situations I had no control over. I never thought I could speak to anyone about the hurt I felt. I was ashamed of my existence. I didn't want people to know that I was a 'mistake' child. The fact that I was introduced to my real father at the age of nine and was a middle child made me feel ashamed that I was born out of wedlock; my other siblings from my mum had the same dad and I could never bring myself to explain to my friends that I had older siblings and younger ones from the same dad.

The insecurities and dissatisfaction of being in my skin were evident. I felt consumed by the shame and confusion of not knowing which family to say was entirely my own. I also thought that I couldn't say I belonged to one family and not the other. It felt like that would mean disowning one set of siblings in favour of the others. I was always envious of the nuclear families that I knew my friends had. I just couldn't face being authentic and often felt I was one person with my friends and another person with my many family members. I couldn't find the gratitude within me to say how lucky I was to have so many siblings that I loved dearly.

CHAPTER 11

The Rage Body

As a teenager, my sub-personality of courage and love became fear and hate. I learnt about sub-personality from researching into the Internal Family System (IFS). It uses Family Systems theory—the idea that individuals cannot be fully understood in isolation from the family unit—to develop techniques and strategies to effectively address issues within a person's internal community or family. This evidence-based approach assumes each individual possesses a variety of sub-personalities, or 'parts,' and attempts to get to know each of these parts better to achieve healing. Parts may be identified as having either healthy and productive roles or extreme roles.[1]

Though my outward demeanor towards most people was that of respect and kindness, I did often get irritable and snappy when I was around my dad. I remember being a smiling, bubbly girl some days, I'd laugh and play with my siblings a lot. On other days, mostly as night fell, I would get agitated and angry, and battle with my aching, tensed body. My earaches and headaches got worse at night. They had almost become a part of me. I stopped telling people I was in pain. I just wanted to be left alone some days. I started to have very little sleep during the nights and I got agitated and felt restless. It was hard for people who knew me as an angry teenager to imagine me as someone who had played joyfully in Martin Shaw Woods. My sense of wonder was lost.

I was sensitive to the slightest of things and had a fear of missing out on anything. I listened to my siblings and my mum talk about some fun times they'd been having in my absence and got jealous. I had FOMO with my friends. I'd get back from studying hard and see them all congregated around their beds, laughing and eating chocolate paste. We usually prepared this by mixing Milo, used to make hot chocolate, and powdered milk with drops of water to make it thick and sticky. I got angry about the fact that they still performed better than me in class or maybe at the same level, even though I almost busted a gut reading over and over again so that I could retain what I read.

I always carried a heavy bag full of books. I'd hold the more massive books in my arms, so they didn't weigh down my shoulders. My peers often saw me walk around with an Ababio Chemistry Textbook and they would shout out, 'Toyin, Toyin, Ababio mama.'

At seventeen years old the only thing I cared deeply about was performing to the highest standards that I knew I had in me to achieve. Even when I wasn't in school, I wore no makeup. The most I'd have would be a little bit of petroleum jelly on my lips and white powder for my face. You wouldn't see me wearing trousers or jeans that would show my body contours in the slightest. I didn't want to attract any boy or man to me. My friends would often call me 'plain Mary', but it didn't bother me. I was more interested in studying hard, but still didn't reap the rewards.

I couldn't stop thinking about the Further Maths test that I'd scored zero in. More poignantly, the voice of my Further Maths teacher was constantly ringing in my head with that question: 'Toyin, is everything OK at home?'

It was the first time I had ever thought intently about how my experiences so far would impact my education or, indeed, my interactions with people. I had simply never made the connection between my experiences and how my brain worked. I never related my life at home to how it might have made my mind freeze on the day of the test. I thought of how this could have correlated with my inability to have a retentive memory. I felt so betrayed by my father.

I couldn't stop thinking about the question my Further Maths teacher had asked me. When I went back to my dad's house for the school holidays, I thought about that question on the plane for an hour until I landed at Lagos Airport.

Two weeks later, it was a Sunday evening just after supper, around 6:30 pm. I was walking down the stairs and caught a whiff of a bad smell. I stopped on the stairway and sniffed. I proceeded to go downstairs, checked the fridge and the cupboards but could find nothing. I could no longer tolerate the persistent smell. I called my siblings and asked them to look for what smelt. They searched, but to no avail.

Frustrated and agitated, I went to get a can of air freshener and began to spray indiscriminately. One of my siblings yelled out, 'Sister Toyin, Dad came down earlier and told us to look for the thing that smelt and not spray.'

We often used the air freshener, but only when we cleaned the house and wanted a fresh fragrant smell to complement the natural scent of the rooms. I knew it made sense not to mask the smell. But the mention of my father's name stirred up a heightened emotion in me. The echoes of the question my Further Maths teacher had asked me rang in my ears. They got louder.

With a sudden rage in my voice and without the fear of consequence I shouted, 'I don't care what he said! We cover everything in this house! What does it matter?'

My siblings' mouths gaped open as they stared at me. My back was to the stairs. I could sense from the look on my siblings' faces that someone was coming down, slowly. I looked behind me, and there stood my dad. He made eye contact with me. He shook his head but said nothing. Then he turned and walked back up the stairs.

My siblings were still in shock. They came to ask if I was OK. They couldn't understand what had brought that on. I just didn't care about anything at that point. I felt robbed, unloved and betrayed by my dad. I went outside and thought about how much I wanted to leave the house for good.

Later that evening, at almost 8 o'clock, it was my turn to lead the prayers. I was feeling a little bit like a hypocrite, having just had an outburst a few hours ago. Still, I had to get one of my siblings to ring the bell and get them all seated in the living room to wait for our dad and my stepmums.

We'd usually plan what message the prayer points would cover for the night. I was ready with my theme; it was going to be verses used in church during the service that day. As a seventeen-year-old, although I was aware that I had been rude, I felt I had been justified, and I hadn't finished making my point.

The passage from the Bible preached in church that morning was taken from 1 John 4: 20. It said, 'If a man says, I love God but hates his brother, he is a liar, for he that loves not his brother whom he hath seen, how can he love God whom he hath not seen?'

We had just finished the praise worship, and I introduced my passage for the night. I started with this line and explained my understanding of it. I explained that being kind to others was much more important than saying you were going to church to prove a point.

My dad quickly stopped me. He added his points to the discussion, saying, 'It's important to go to church.'

Although I hadn't finished, I knew he wanted me to stop because I was steering the discussion towards him. Of course, I was only going to say this implicitly. I sensed an officiousness to his tone; he'd brushed me aside.

The anger I felt almost exploded in me. I thought of walking out of the prayer session, but I sat down. I didn't want to let my siblings down by storming out. They looked up to me, and I'd always spoken to them about showing respect to everyone.

They'd already seen a bit of my angry sub-personality, so I stayed composed. I often felt silenced and inauthentic, under pressure to carry on being the model big sister that people expected me to be. The heaviness of this burden weighed me down.

I always felt overly burdened with the expectation that I had to be strong for my siblings and be a perfect role model. I was the second eldest, the first girl out of a total of twelve of us from my dad's side. Ever since I'd come to Nigeria, I'd always shown great interest in my siblings' needs from both my mum's and dad's side. Most of my siblings often joked and called me 'Iya kekere wa' (our little mum). I didn't mind it at all, but I never shared my feelings. They didn't know how much pain I was hiding. When I went to visit my other half siblings and Mum, she often gave me the responsibility of stepping into her shoes when she went to social gatherings or when she went to work. I felt I couldn't express my needs or my worries. I stopped speaking of my pain because of the expectations placed on me. I assumed a mother's role to those around me, even my friends! I put myself on a high pedestal too, because I was older than all of my friends.

We finished the prayer session, and I stayed in the living room. I talked to my siblings and told them that I was just generally not in a good mood. I hugged them. I explained my erratic behaviour to them and how we all got like that sometimes. I didn't tell them the real reason for my outburst. My rage stemmed from my father possibly being partially responsible for the reason I scored zero out of a hundred in my Further Maths test, and my resentment towards him during the church service that morning. For you to understand a little bit more about my frustration, I'll have to take you back to what happened that morning.

Sunday mornings were often busy times in our house. There was always a lot of noise in the house as everyone rushed to get ready to go to our Anglican church service. There was no enforced legislation regarding polygamy in our parish in Nigeria (or at least it didn't appear so, since my father had two wives). My stepmums would wake early to cook the popular and delicious Nigerian breakfast; yam and egg stew, with fried peppers and onions. I got up to help them before I dressed for church. I was planning to walk to church because, apart from it only being about fifteen minutes' walk, I wasn't in the mood to travel with my dad.

He noticed I was ready to leave before him, and he asked why I wasn't waiting for the rest of the family. I recall being snappy and said I'd dressed and was ready to go. I left and got to church at almost the same time the rest of the family did. My dad would drive himself to church in the Cressida, he also had a big and spacious Mitsibushi van, big enough to get all of us in it and driven by one of his drivers when we had to go to church or other places. We usually had our set place to sit down, and most church members knew this. We were a well-known family; my dad was a church warden and a very well-respected man in the church community. It was not unusual for church members to go out of their way to greet our father. Two men that my dad hadn't seen for some time walked up to him and prostrated. My dad beamed with a broad smile and said, 'Haaa, oju yin rey, shey dada ni' (It's been a while, how are you?).

The men replied, 'Adupe sir, beh ni sir, eku ijo meta, sir' (We are well thank you, sir. Yes, sir, it's been a little while, sir.).

The mere fact that the men repeatedly said 'sir' at the end of every phrase annoyed me so much. I walked past them all, brushing shoulders against one of the men, and went into the church to sit down.

As we all got up to sing the entry song, I watched my father walk into the church carrying the brass stave with a cross at the tip. He, alongside another warden, was behind the archdeacon. I couldn't take my eyes off my dad as he strolled in a holy and humble manner towards the pulpit and bowed with his officiating partner. I felt bitterness towards him. I thought of him as a hypocrite and couldn't understand why God wouldn't make that staff turn into a snake and strike at him.

I remember watching him intently during the church service and feeling indignant, hurt and in deep pain. But the feeling of betrayal was more profound; I'd never been this enraged before. Throughout the service, my mind wandered. Once the service was over, he demanded that I travelled in the car back home with him and a few of my siblings came along, others travelled in the Mitsubishi. I said nothing as he and the others chatted all the way home. All I could think of was how easy for him to be such a sham.

I then thought of what I had shamefully done just two weeks ago, before we'd broken up from school. My friends and I were in the dormitory just outside the Quadrangle. We were chatting about all sorts when Fisayo said, 'Toyin is so lucky!'

I looked at her and said, 'Why do you say that?'

'Well, you're daddy's girl, aren't you?'

Slowly but thoughtfully, I said, 'Please don't say that.'

She looked at me and said, 'What do you mean, "I shouldn't say that"? You have a driver that drops you and picks you up from mine. Your dad even has a pet name for you. What's it again? Oh, I remember, TJ.'

Before she could finish her sentence, I pounced on her. I dragged her towards the toilet and punched her repeatedly, pinning her to the wall. It was like an out-of-body experience. I didn't stop hitting her, and she was in utter shock! She was protecting her face but could barely defend herself. Other girls rushed to us, pulling me away and shouting, 'Toyin! Stop! What is wrong with you?!'

I was breathless and looked at my friend, who could barely say a word. I stormed off to the toilet and cried. I was angry with myself. I was disappointed by what I had just done. I had never fought in my whole life before that incident. I just couldn't bear being called 'daddy's girl'. I snapped!

We didn't speak to each other for days. Our other close friends talked us out of the grudge bearing. I couldn't bring myself to explain to her why I hated being called daddy's girl. While I did apologise for my erratic behaviour, I also said she should have stopped teasing me when I told her to. Still, I knew my actions were not justified.

The holiday period got worse over the next few weeks. I was determined to be on top of my game the following term when we resumed school so I'd brought my Further Maths textbook home. One of my stepmums had a very brainy nephew; his name was Akeem. We were in the same year, so I usually got him to teach me Maths and Further Maths when he came over to see his cousins.

We were three weeks into the summer holidays and he'd come over, so I thought I'd seize the opportunity to ask him to go through last term's topics in Further Maths with me. Akeem was a very calm and collected boy. Everyone took a liking to him because he was polite, courteous and funny. Our dad always admired his calm demeanour. I saw him as my cousin too.

On that particular day, it was around 12:30 pm. I'd just finished cleaning my room and we were settling down, getting ready for him to teach me. I'd asked him in my bedroom since I had a big study table, and there would be no distractions from my siblings. He whisked through the topics and gave me a brief overview before he dived in more in-depth. He was a natural and I understood everything he explained. We were working on the final topic for the day when we heard my dad's horn at the gate. I was surprised that he was back from work so early. It was around 3 pm. I then remembered him mentioning that morning that he had a conference in the evening at Eko Hotel in Victoria Island, Lagos. Akeem and I continued working, and one of my siblings opened the gate for the driver to come through with my dad. As I was working through a question, my dad burst into my room. Before Akeem and I could say 'Welcome home' to him, he started yelling at me.

'Why is Akeem in your room?' he shouted.

I was shocked by his attitude and felt embarrassed and angry at the same time. With a confused look, I pointed at the books and, before I could say a word, he came at me and slapped me so hard across the face that I hit my head against my bed. I couldn't believe my eyes. Akeem was in utter shock and said, 'Ema Binu, sir.' (Please don't be angry, sir.)

My dad stormed out of my room as I held my face, still dazed and confused as to why he had slapped me. Akeem apologised, even though he had done nothing wrong. He left my room swiftly.

I went to my father at around 6 pm. I was still furious. I shouted, 'Why did you slap me?'

He looked at me as if to say, *How dare you ask me that question?*

'You should never let boys into your room!' he shouted. 'You're a girl!'

I took one look at him, then shook my head and walked out of his room. I slammed the door behind me.

The next day was Saturday. I woke up early, around 5 am. I'd packed a few of my clothes the night before. I went to have a quick shower and was mindful not to wake anyone up, particularly my father. Once I'd finished and had got dressed, I picked up my packed bag and a few books and tiptoed downstairs. I walked slowly and cautiously to the gate and carefully slid the side door open. As soon as I was outside, my pace increased. I ran as fast as I could to the back end of our house so that I didn't risk the chance of anyone seeing me through the windows upstairs.

It was around 6 am, and I wanted to be out of the area while it was still dark. I got on a bus and headed straight to my stepdad's and my siblings' house. I arrived there around 7:45 am. I rang the doorbell non-stop until I could hear the voice of Auntie Bola, my stepdad's relative, shouting, 'Tani yehn?' (Who is that?)

She looked through the peephole on the door and said, 'Ah-ah! Basirat, shey Iwo ni yeh?' (Basirat, is that you?). Everyone on my stepdad's side still called me Basirat.

I said, 'Yes, please open the door.'

Once I was in, I didn't wait for Auntie Bola to ask me why I was there so early. I shouted, 'I'm never going back there!'

She was confused and asked me to sit down. I explained to her about the incident with Akeem and how my dad had slapped me. She was shocked. She laughed angrily and pointed at me saying, 'You're joking. Your dad slapped you!'

She knew I was generally well behaved and couldn't understand why anyone would slap me. I'd never got beaten before. I very rarely got told off when I was with my stepdad, mum and siblings.

Our mum had travelled back to the UK early that year, in 1989, and wasn't planning to return. She wrote to us all regularly and sent my siblings and I a lot of clothing, money and other lovely unique items that were too expensive or difficult to get hold of in Nigeria. She and my stepdad had separated. I often blamed myself for their separation. But, like any separation, there were a lot of contributing factors to it. Their separation was no different.

My stepdad had gone to his hometown to visit his sister. While my siblings were on holiday with relatives, Auntie Bola was looking after the house until they all returned. They were going to be away for the next two weeks.

I explained to her that I never wanted to go back home and asked if I could stay with them all. She looked at me and wasn't sure how to answer. I think she also thought it wasn't her place to say yes or no. She knew it must have been serious for me to have run away from home and said, 'Sure, sure, you know you're always welcome.'

I settled down, and we had a long discussion about everything that had been going on at home since the start of the summer holiday.

After a week, my aunt sat me down and said I should reconsider going back home. She told me that my dad and everyone else would be worried about my whereabouts. I attempted to tell her the real reason I was furious with my father and why I hated him so much, but I just couldn't. I made several attempts to tell her throughout the one and a half weeks that I was with her, but I couldn't find the words. I felt drowned in a 'hushed' state.

I'd been at my stepdad and siblings' house for a week and a half when Auntie Bola convinced me to go back home. She said she'd take me back. I thought about it, and since most of my things were still at home, especially my passport, it made sense to go. We went the next day. On the way back home, I was getting a little scared. I also felt that I should have told Auntie Bola the real reason, but I said nothing.

We arrived home, and all my siblings shouted out my name. They were so pleased to see me. They got emotional. My dad came outside and, before he could say anything, Auntie Bola knelt, pulling me down to kneel with her. She apologised to my dad on my behalf and said I wouldn't run away again. I didn't look him in the eye. I said I was sorry without making eye contact. I hugged Auntie Bola, and she left. She didn't want to go in the house. I could sense she was angry with my father.

My dad didn't bring up the issue of me running away. It was like I'd never left. I was happy he didn't, but my feelings towards him were unchanged. All I could think of was the real reason I hated him. From that day onwards, I'd lay in bed thinking how things could have been different.

CHAPTER 12

God Doesn't Care!

For you to know why I hated my father so much, I'll have to take you back to when I was twelve years old. I had just been accepted into the school my dad wanted me to attend. It was Command Secondary School, in the high and cold mountain city of Jos. I was petrified of going to such a regimented army school and remember thinking how strict this school would be. I thought how far I would be from my home in Lagos and wondered if I would make good friends that 'got me', people who, like me, had come over from Lagos and not just from the locality of the city of Jos, where their culture might be somewhat different to mine. Yet I also knew that it was a school that I would proudly boast of to my family and friends back home. It was quite a prestigious school and held some kind of clout. I had warmed up to what my dad had explained to me about the current government regime of Nigeria being military at the time. Although I was still nervous about all the unknowns that a military boarding school entailed, I knew I would be on my best behaviour and might not have to worry too much about being flogged. Still, it was an unknown that often made me feel tight in the chest.

Although the school term was due to start in September, my father took me to Jos in June to be introduced to the Commandant (equivalent to the Headteacher of secondary schools) and to get me to familiarise myself with the whole environment. Here I refer to my birth father, my biological father. (I feel the emphasis is essential here since I had three fathers in my life.) The one I got introduced to by my mother at the age of nine when we went on the long bus ride, the father who exclaimed that I had his eyes. The one I started living with when I turned twelve.

He had secured accommodation for us at the Tati Hotel. The rain bore down mercilessly upon the heart of the city as we travelled to the hotel. It pounded down on the streets.

Later that night, in the hotel room, I felt the weight, the heaviness of something on my little body. In fright, I remember opening my eyes, and seeing a familiar face, a face that should have been protecting me, protecting me from harm.

I looked up and saw my father. I froze. My father was violating me. When he left my room I didn't cry, I didn't know what to think. I didn't sleep. I couldn't sleep.

I got up and went to have a shower, it was around 3.00am. When I finished, I went back to bed.

My eyes were fixed on the ceiling. I witnessed the day break. I hadn't had a wink of sleep. I felt shaky but too scared to cry.

I remembered how I used to sob after I left Ratby in Leicester. I remembered back then at eight when I said, 'I hate my life. This is the worst ever, and I don't want this life.'

I'd thought that leaving my foster family at the tender age of eight was my rock bottom, that I would never live past the pain. But now something worse had happened.

I usually prayed and read my Bible before bedtime, and when I woke up in the mornings. I'd started that routine at the age of nine when I'd become a Christian. When I got up that morning in the hotel, I looked at the Bible on my bedside table and said, 'God doesn't care! I'm not reading the Bible. I hate God!'

I pushed it onto the floor with great force. I didn't understand how I was feeling. I picked it up again. I was scared that God might punish me. I held the Bible and then placed it back on the side table. I went to have another shower, around 7:00 a.m. When I'd finished I sat on the floor, still in the bathroom. I ran through everything that I had endured so far; it was like I was looking at my life's timeline of horrible events. I snapped out of my thoughts. I knew I had to be downstairs for breakfast. I stood up, quickly rinsed and stepped out of the shower. I sat on the bed, holding my bathrobe tight to my body. I knew I was late for breakfast now. I didn't want my dad to come to my room, so I jumped up quickly and started dressing. He came and banged on the door. He shouted and said I should hurry up and meet him downstairs for breakfast. I remember shaking; I was too scared to cry. I didn't reply. I wanted to believe that everything in my head was a nightmare and that nothing had happened the night before. But it had.

I went down for breakfast, where I was met by a lady friend of my dad's, who also sat down to have breakfast with us. For some reason, I was glad she was there because she took away the awkwardness of me having to sit with him alone. I recall staring at the bowl of cornflakes, and I didn't even have a spoonful of it.

The lady noticed. 'Toyin, you'll be OK at school,' she said. 'Are you nervous about going to a military school?'

Not that I was eager to answer, but before I could attempt to say anything, my dad said, 'There's nothing to be nervous about.'

Everything after that hotel experience was a blur. We all left the hotel and went to school. Though I was being asked a lot of questions by the Vice Principal at the time, I barely uttered a word. My dad responded to most, if not all, of the questions. We left for Lagos late that afternoon, and I didn't utter a word throughout the hour-long journey back, even though he was talking to me as if everything was normal.

That day back in the hotel in Jos was the beginning of my worst days. The abuse continued at home; I was sexually abused by my father from twelve years old until I was fifteen. I was abused for three long, agonising years. I decided I could no longer go on. Life and death stood face to face, but I chose life.

The metaphor of the air freshener masking the smell was what stirred up the emotions in me that day years later. I thought at the time, *Here we are saying we should look for the smell and not cover it up, yet my father has covered up his abuse towards me. What a hypocrite!*

Throughout that time, my foster mum was the rainbow in my clouds. My foster family was the rainbow in my clouds. Everyone who showed me love, in Ratby, was the rainbow in my clouds. I thought of them every day after that incident, and knew I had to carry on. They would have been distraught if they got to know that I didn't give faith a fighting chance.

My loved ones' grief would have been profound, asking themselves why I had never said anything, how they could have had no idea. But no one understands unless you've been through it, the shock and unspoken silence that eats up a child. No one can understand the fight or freeze mode and the inescapable shock. No one understands the ultimate 'hush' and shame that a child feels. It's something words cannot explain.

I thought about how my little life would be remembered if I didn't choose life.

I drew strength from my foster mum. I tried to disempower the negative thoughts that came to my mind so often. I missed her so much. I knew if I was going to have any chance of seeing her again, I would have to live. We all have rainbows in our clouds; there's always someone out there that loves you and wants you to keep your sense of wonder. For me, it was my foster family. I couldn't sit it out – I had to participate in life's experience. Yes, it was as if I did feel those mountains in the distance, but I had to climb higher, I had to travel further. I faced terrifying situations and thought, 'My life is not worth living. How would I know?' I had to live to find out.

PART IV

HEALING

CHAPTER 13

Inner Child Healing Begins

My foster family certainly played a big part in how I pulled through. There were a lot of unintentional healing processes that I embarked on to get by. The first unintentional healing journey was watching *The Sound of Music*. It remains my favourite film of all time. Thank you, Julie Andrews, thank you, Christopher Plummer, and thank you to all the cast who played the children that I became immersed in and superimposed myself onto (even the boys), depending on my mood.

I watched *The Sound of Music* almost once a fortnight from when I was introduced to it by my biological father in the first week I moved in to live with him and his family. The first time I watched the film, I took one look at Maria (Julie Andrews) and found myself edging in slowly, moving right up to the telly. I became fully immersed and my world became one with this movie. Each time I watched *The Sound of Music* my imagination ran deep. I superimposed the image of Maria onto my foster mum. As Maria sang, I closed my eyes and said, 'Mum is singing to me right now.' I added more imaginative scenes to the film and imagined her saying, 'Bas, remember always to be polite. Keep your face clean and remember to be humble and kind to everyone.' I felt my foster mum was singing to me. I customised the words, saying she would add more phrases to the chats and advice she gave me. From when I was thirteen onwards, she would quote lyrics from songs by Lee Ann Womack and Gladys Knight that referred to dancing through everything in life. She might say, 'When you feel fed up with it all, don't give up, me duck.'

As I sang the lyrics from *The Sound of Music* – about climbing over all the mountains that came our way – I felt tears running down my cheeks. It felt like there were so many more mountains to climb, but the song felt real because it was sung by a white woman that I related to my foster mum. I had trust and faith in her. She never let me down. I felt closer to the UK, and unknowingly, it was therapeutic to me. I danced as I sang.

As I danced, I expressed myself fully. It replaced what I didn't say in words. I had big 'pity parties', crying as I sang, feeling sorry for 'little Bas' and 'young Toyin'.

There is a lot of recent research into the rewiring of our brains with neuroplasticity. Dancing has shown many health benefits, including boosting brainpower and function[1].

I had always enjoyed drawing pictures, from the age of around five. By the time I was twelve, I'd become an avid drawer. I drew because it was a way for me to put on paper what was hurting me beyond words, and it was a matter of necessity.

In secondary school, when I was around fourteen, I scored a low mark in Integrated Science (This was a unified subject that combined physics, chemistry and biology.). We'd been asked to draw a housefly, but the teacher said I had traced my picture. I was in tears, pleading with her to check the textbook. My drawing was larger than the one in the book. I couldn't have traced it. She took no notice of my tears. I scored 4 out of 10 for my drawing, mistaken for a traced piece of art.

Although I had a lot of friends, and I seemed present, I still felt isolated and alone. These were the times I sought comfort in drawing. I continued to draw even when I started higher education. I attended the Federal Polytechnic, Ilaro, Ogun state in Nigeria, and it was around two hours' drive from Lagos. I studied Accounting at the Ordinary National Diploma level. My father wanted me to become a doctor, but I didn't get the grades to study Medical Science.

Again I wasn't performing to the best of my ability. I had a lot of friends and studied night and day, but was an average student. Attending the polytechnic was fun because I stayed away from home most of the time. My close friend was Tutu, and we shared a room off campus. We cooked most of our meals together and were like sisters. Tutu was a fantastic friend. At one point I contracted typhoid fever while at the polytechnic. It was debilitating. I remember waking up in the morning and not being able to move. I was weak and ached all over. I didn't eat or drink anything. It was after three days that Tutu rushed me to the clinic at school. The symptoms got worse, so she took me home. On the way home, she realised I was falling in and out of consciousness, so she took me straight to the hospital. I got immediately placed on a drip. The doctors said I was lucky and praised my friend for her quick and smart thinking. Tutu then rushed to my house to inform my family. My father and stepmum came to the hospital to see me almost lifeless. It was a terrifying experience. I am forever grateful to Tutu for taking the quick and lifesaving steps that she took. I lost more than half of my body weight and returned to the polytechnic after two weeks. I was barely recognisable and had to use safety pins on all my skirts to keep them from slipping down.

While I was at the polytechnic, I started to map out how I was going to travel back to the UK. I couldn't stand staying with my father any longer. Returning to the UK wasn't as easy as it should have been, even though I was a citizen. My name change was going to be the biggest hurdle; proving I was indeed a British citizen, I knew, would be difficult for me to prove since my name was now completely different to the one on my passport. I was in my final year of studying a part-time three-year Ordinary National Diploma programme in 1995; I was twenty-three. My father was seeking ways for me to go to the Higher National Diploma (the upper end to the Polytechnic programme). Polytechnics are classified as institutions at a level below universities. Although once you finish studying at the HND class, you apply for a job the same way university graduates do, employers often favour university graduates over polytechnic candidates. A lot of HND graduates consider crossing over to universities to get a degree.

I had no intention of continuing my education in Nigeria after my OND. I had had enough. The resentment towards my father grew every day. I remember feeling like a hypocrite when I allowed him to throw me a big twenty-first birthday party. I couldn't live the pretence anymore.

He had my passport in his room, so I started planning how I was going to 'steal' it and start the whole renewal process. My mum and all my half-siblings that I'd come to Nigeria with had returned to the UK. My mum worked hard when she went back to the UK in 1989, often doing two or more jobs. She sent money to my siblings for them to renew their passports and buy flight tickets for them to join her in the UK. My stepdad consented to her having them with her. Since I lived with my father and he was now in charge of all my affairs, it wasn't easy for my mum to ask my dad to let me join her in the UK. He exercised a great level of control over all his children. Besides that, she 'knew' that my dad was providing me with all the education I needed; he was well-off and she knew he would, at some point, let me return to the UK. She did not know, at this point, the abuse that I had endured. I hadn't told anyone about it. Knowing that the rest of my half-siblings had returned to the UK made me feel even more different and anxious.

I was responsible for tidying my father's bedroom regularly when he went to work. He often locked the door to his room. On the day I planned to 'steal' my passport, I asked him to leave his door unlocked for me to clean it. As soon as he left for work, I went straight to his room and looked for my passport.

I searched everywhere, being mindful not to leave anything out of place. My father always knew the positioning of all his things, even the tiniest notepad.

Finally! I found it. I rushed back to my room, shutting my eyes and holding it close to my chest. I was so excited to have it in my hands. But I knew I still had one more hurdle to climb. My passport still had my old name. I needed the paper where the affidavit indicated my name change. I immediately thought I would never be able to travel and thought out loud, 'Even with the correct details, it's hard enough convincing the British Embassy sixteen years after leaving the UK that I am who I say I am on the passport, but with a complete name change?'

I was getting deflated and discouraged, but I was going to give it my all. When I finally got myself composed, I had to work out a plan. I went back to my dad's room to look for the paper and supporting documents that stated my name change to Oluwatoyin Balogun. I found them quite easily. I now had to figure out how this was all going to work out. I got in touch with my biological mum in the UK and explained that I needed proof of my name change.. She said she would get in touch with Mr and Mrs Kind and Ratby Primary so they could provide proof that I was indeed the same person indicated on the passport. I wasn't very hopeful.

I was ecstatic when, in just less than a month, I got a message from my mum through an aunt, enclosing a letter from my foster dad! When I saw his writing, I burst into tears. I felt so close to him, and I knew I was on my way back to the UK. My foster dad's letter read:

Dear Sir/Madam,
My wife and I fostered the lady concerned from when she was two months old until she was eight, from 1972 to 1980. We understand that before her changing to secondary school, her natural father changed her name. 'Bas' – as we knew her – was a member of our family and we would be delighted to have her back, and sincerely hope this letter will be of assistance.
Yours faithfully,
Mr Kind

I didn't put the passport back in my dad's room but made sure the brown envelope that I took it out of was bulked up as if there was something in it. I didn't know if he'd check in it or not, but I wasn't going to risk putting my passport back in his room. I placed it in one of my suitcases, locked it up and pushed the case behind a lot of other cases under my bed. I took the key everywhere with me! On 16th January 1995, I went to the British High Commission to renew my passport. My heart was racing as I waited to get seen, I remember sitting and watching everyone in the waiting room who, like me, looked fretful. When it was my turn, I looked at the white lady behind the counter and I immediately felt at ease. I handed my documents over to her, and she smiled, received my payment of N720.00, and gave me a receipt.

3rd July 1995 and I went back to the British High Commission for my interview for the processing of my passport. I sat in the waiting area with butterflies dancing in my tummy. When I got called, the lady simply smiled, handed me my renewed passport and said, 'You must be so excited to go back to see your foster family in the UK.' I screamed and had tears flowing down my face. I thought to myself, 'If only she knew my journey over the past sixteen years!'

My foster dad's letter, as well as a letter from Ratby School with a few photos, was sufficient to prove who I was when I presented them at the embassy.

Again, I was so grateful to my foster parents. They facilitated the process of ensuring that I had all the necessary documentation to make the renewal of my passport a success.

It was September 1995 and I was twenty-three years old. I only told my dad I was planning to return to the UK when I had finished the whole passport renewal process. I told him I was leaving in a few months. He was in utter disbelief. I wasn't going to tell him until I'd finished the whole renewal process because I couldn't risk him asking me to hand over the passport and I felt I'd never see the passport again if I chanced asking his permission. It was easier to ask for forgiveness than to seek permission. I told him that I would ask my mum to send me money for a plane ticket so he didn't think I was expecting him to pay; I said I would let him know when I'd be leaving. In disbelief, he nodded his head and said, 'I'll miss you.' At that point, I felt like pouring my heart out to him as a final way of saying he destroyed me. But I was not bold enough.. Instead, I sighed and went to my room. I had attempted to confront my biological father on several occasions. I just never had the guts. The 'hushed state' was intense; I felt like he had caged me like a trapped bird. My mind felt enslaved and not my own. I felt he still had control over me, even though I was taking bold steps to be free from him.

Before I left for the UK, I wanted to tell someone what I'd gone through so that they would know the real person my father was. I confided in a trusted relative, an aunt from my dad's side of the family. She had come over to visit on a Saturday so I asked if we could go for a walk. I said I wanted to tell her something and I didn't want anyone at home to hear us. As we walked down the road, hand in hand, I looked up at her and, before she could even ask me what I wanted to tell her, I blurted out, 'He sexually abused me for over three years.'

She looked at me, let go of my hand, and, with both hands, held my shoulders, shaking them as she asked, 'Who?'

Tears filled my eyes. I felt ashamed, angry and in pain, but relieved for unburdening myself of what I had carried for almost eleven years. I was now twenty-three and my father had abused me for three years – from the age of twelve until I was around fifteen. I had never told anyone. I closed my eyes and said, 'Daddy.'

Tears filled her eyes as she gently drew me close to her and away from the middle of the walkway. She held me close to her chest and said, 'Please tell me it's not true, please. No. No. No.'

We both said nothing. As tears rolled down my cheeks, I felt the muscles of my chin tremble like a small child. I felt a slight lightness in my chest.

We walked back home, and I told her to promise me she'd never tell anyone. With a deep nod, and her eyes closed, she wiped away her tears. With a deep intake of breath and a slow release, she said, 'OK, I promise.'

I knew I needed to have a heart-to-heart with my stepdad before I returned to the UK in a few months. I had not seen him in a while, due to being at boarding school. My stepfather spent most of his time visiting relatives in his hometown and would often stay there for months at a time. There were so many unanswered questions that I had held in my heart over the years. Although I had written several letters to him, I was never bold enough to send them. I wrote them, cried and cried and then simply ripped them up. But now I was ready to meet him face to face.

I got up early in the morning, at around 4 am. It was always easy for me to wake up early. I'd stopped having deep sleep since I left Ratby back in the UK. My sleep pattern got worse over time; I could hardly sleep through the night by that point. My heart was pumping; my head racing with questions I wanted to ask him. At that stage, I hadn't seen or spoken to him for over six years. A relative informed me that he'd left Lagos and now lived in Oyo state, an inland state in south-western Nigeria. All the questions I wanted clarification on kept popping up. Memories were now awakening, memories that I'd never forgotten. Suddenly I felt I was forced to swim once more in the tidewaters of the past. These questions I was so desperate to get answers to were like competing speech balloons in the air, all fighting to jump out first.

'Did you know I wasn't your daughter?'

'Why was I your "little girl" even though you knew I wasn't your daughter?'

'Did you think of the implications of me meeting my dad when I did?'

'Were you and Mum going to keep me a secret?'

'Did my real dad contact you or Mum to demand his daughter?'

'Did you think it was a good idea for you and Mum not to tell me sooner?'

'Did you know when Mum took me to see my real dad for the first time?'

'Did both of you discuss it?'

I needed closure on all these questions. I didn't want to feel anger towards my stepdad the way I did because I wanted to believe that he must have been hurting too. Yet I wasn't sure if he was. I knew the love he had for me was real, and seeing me go must have cut deep in his heart the way it did mine (or at least I hoped it did) and I wanted reassurance that he did love me and was going to miss me.

It was a very long three-and-a-half-hour journey through heavy traffic on the Lagos—Ibadan expressway to the southern part of the city, Oyo state. As I boarded the bus at around 9:15 am, I was greeted by mothers who, in addition to having heavy loads of bags filled with different foods, also had their babies strapped to their backs with old African print fabric – *ankara*. It was tightly packed and suffocating on the bus, and I soon found myself occupying half a seat when a woman squeezed her three-year-old child next to me.

My head was as unsteady as the instability and rickety movement of the bus as it travelled into the city. My head was racing. I was tired, both physically and mentally. The sun's never-ending rays beat down on me mercilessly. Salty sweat rolled off my forehead, stinging my eyes. Plumes of dust erupted as the wind stirred up the wispy sand. The great swirls of dust made their way through the opened windows. My clothes were overwhelmingly hot and sticky.

As I got closer to my stepdad's house, I felt my pulse pounding in my temples. All my preparations had fled my mind like a scared child. My brain was static. The scenarios I had constructed got lost in the discomfort of the travel on the bus and the nervous emotions I was feeling.

I got to his house around 12:30 pm. As I approached the door, I wiped the sweat off my face. It was a combination of nervousness and the scorching heat. He opened the door and looked at me in complete shock.

'Daddy!' I said.

He gave me a slightly confused look and said, 'Basirat?'

I was still Basirat to him.

'Beh ni sir,' (That's right) I said as I knelt.

Without asking why I had come so far, he flung his arms open. He wasn't expecting me. Back then, you simply made these long trips, praying that you'd meet the person at home. There were no mobile phones, and I didn't have his home telephone number as I had lost all contact with him. My half-siblings and mum had all returned to the UK. There was no way I could get in touch with him before the visit.

I was exhausted. I'd never made such a trip in my life! My dad's driver took me most places. I hadn't informed my dad that I was going to see my stepdad. He wouldn't have approved of me going. I wasn't prepared to get into an argument with him if he did refuse. I can't remember my dad ever speaking of my stepdad so I was sure they were not in contact. I had to find my own way. I lied to my father that I was going to pack up my things at the polytechnic. I had just finished my final year of OND. I said I didn't want to disturb Baba Ramo since I was leaving early. My father said it was OK. Ever since I'd informed him of my plans to return to the UK, he rarely said no to my demands. I guess he didn't see the point.

Once my stepdad and I finished our initial chat, I sat down briefly. My mouth was dry. I panted from the heat. It was a thirst like I'd never known before. My saliva was thick like wallpaper paste. I licked my lips, trying to wet my mouth. Without saying a word, he went to the kitchen to get me a refreshing bottle of coke. I closed my eyes gently as I savoured the drink. I drank gulps and gulps at a time. It stung my throat, but I couldn't stop. I needed to quench my burning thirst.

We sat and spoke for hours on end. My stepdad asked how I was, and we both exchanged the customary greetings. My stepdad knew I hadn't come all the way to chat about everyday things. I apologised for not having stayed in touch with him for so long and complimented him on how well he looked. He reached out to hold my hand and explained how much he had missed me. He said a day never went by without him thinking of me. He was emotional.

After a long chat, we had rice and chicken that was in his fridge. Although I was enjoying his company and I would have loved to stay a lot longer, I was conscious of the time, I couldn't bear the thought of travelling the road late at night, and the thought of making the dreaded three-hour journey back to Lagos kept crossing my mind.

I started to steer our conversation slightly towards the questions that had brought me all this way. We had already begun to touch on my childhood a little, so it felt right to start asking those questions. I got consumed by the long story he told me about how distraught he was when Mum took me to get introduced to my dad. He was implicitly answering most of the questions. He said he knew the transition wasn't handled well but that he'd got caught up in his feelings of losing me. He said he'd left it to my mum to deal with. He told me that he knew I wasn't his daughter a few months after I was born, but wasn't sure my real dad knew about me. With glistening eyes he said, 'Basirat, I never saw you as not being my daughter. I had forgiven your mum, and we had both decided that we would bring you up as my daughter.'

All that changed, he explained, when word got out and someone my mum had confided in told my biological father. At that point, all I could think of was what I had endured with my biological dad. But I was never going to tell my stepdad about the sexual abuse I endured, I didn't see the point and it would undoubtedly have destroyed my stepdad.

It was a soul-healing visit. I spoke to him about most of the things that had been burning inside me when I left him all those years ago. At that point, I felt a weight of trauma drop off my shoulders. I felt great relief, knowing that he loved me. When I told him I would be travelling to the UK in a few months, we hugged and both became emotional. We both knew that it might be the last time we'd see each other.

It was the last time. I spoke to my stepdad a few times after I returned to the UK and he passed away in 2006. He was seventy-seven.

I felt healed in part when I went to see my stepdad. I will always be grateful for the part he played in my life. It was a short but loving life that we shared. Expressing my hurt and pain to him was satisfying.

After the visit to my stepdad, I felt ready to travel back to the UK. Although I still felt the need to confront my biological dad, I didn't. A few days before it was time for me to travel, I called my siblings together and gave all my clothes, shoes and other belongings to all four of my sisters. I gave my brothers and sisters some money and told them to be good. I didn't tell any of them about the abuse, but I hoped that since their mum was in the house and they slept in the same room as they did, our dad would not hurt them. Our father had a place for himself. Still, I told my sisters to look after themselves, and to tell their mum anything that upset them.

I had grown so fond of my half-siblings on my dad's side. I always felt responsible for all ten that were younger than me. Their mums knew they all looked up to me. I often wondered if my stepmums were aware of the abuse I'd endured, but I never found out whether they had any idea. I did want to tell my stepmums, but I didn't. To a great extent, I felt ashamed and thought they might get too angry and confront my dad. I didn't want to be the cause of a break-up between them and my dad.

I would put on a brave face most of the time for them to see my strengths and not my weaknesses. The truth was, beneath my brave face was hidden pain.

My dad's driver brought my father and most of my siblings to see me off at the Murtala Muhammed International Airport in Lagos on 20th January 1996. It was an emotional departure. I hugged everyone before I walked through to the departure area. I looked back, waving until I could no longer see them.

It was a six-hour flight from Lagos to London Heathrow. It had been sixteen years since I'd left for Nigeria in 1980. I couldn't wait to go to Leicester.

I was picked up by my half-sister and her boyfriend. I was so happy to see my sister. Though I was looking forward to seeing my biological mum, who had returned to the UK in 1989, I couldn't stop thinking about my reunion with my foster family. My mum now lived in London and was working two different jobs in the public sector. She was busy working to make sure we all had everything provided for us, whilst securing her own future as a single parent. Though she worked hard to provide us with the physical things we needed, I often felt her absence emotionally. My mum had a lot of friends and was loved by many she came into contact with. She was always generous to those that came into contact with her. She would often help strangers and become close friends with them. My mum later explained that the reason I was suddenly taken away from my foster family, back in 1980, was because my grandparents, on my stepdad's side, were desperate to see me and my siblings. They were not sure whether or not they would get to see us all before they passed away. My mum said the whole move was sudden to her too. It was my stepdad's parents that demanded we came to Nigeria, and my mum went with what her in-laws wanted.

My mum was excited to see me. We hugged and I talked to her and my sister for ages. I hadn't told either of them about the abuse while they were still in Nigeria. I wasn't ready to say anything to them at that point, either. As soon as I was settled at my mum's house, I got my foster family's number and rang them immediately. Mum was ecstatic! I couldn't believe I was listening to her sweet voice. She handed the phone over to my foster dad. He was emotional.

'Oh, Bas,' he said. 'I can't believe it's you!'

Above left: Dad Kind me and mum Kind
Above right: Reunited - Me and my sister, Paula

We arranged for me to visit them in Leicester. They still lived in the same house next to Martin Shaw Woods. Most of my foster sisters and brother had their own families, so I went over when the whole family was present.

When I got to Leicester, I got picked up by all of my foster siblings, foster mum and dad! It was the best day ever. We couldn't stop chatting in the car, and I remember Andrew, my foster brother, asking me why I hadn't replied to all the letters. Mum asked if I'd received the necklace she sent. I couldn't believe they never got my messages, and I never received any of theirs. It was comforting to know they did send me letters, even though I never received them.

My birth parents never sent my letters, and when they received some from my foster parents, they decided it was best not to give them to me. They did what they thought was the right thing to do at the time. I guess when we know better, we do better.

When we got home, I was greeted by balloons and a large banner hanging outside the house. The banner read: 'Welcome home Bas'. I was overwhelmed. We got inside and I couldn't stop looking around. My pictures were just as they were, before I left sixteen years ago. I was so emotional; I was filled with peace and joy.

Top left, from the left, Paula, Carolyn, my niece, Natalie – Carloyn's daughter; me and Julie.

Top right: Arriving home after sixteen years of leaving for Nigeria, and was greeted by balloons and a large "Welcome Home Bas" banner.

Bottom left: Me and mum Kind.

Bottom right: A welcome Home Bas" cake.

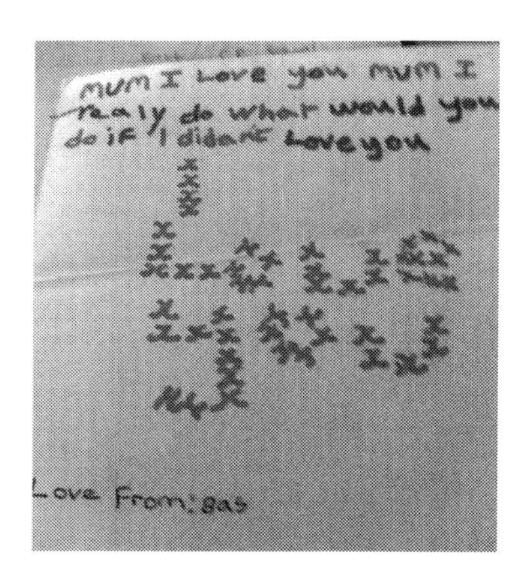

mum I love you mum I
realy do what would you
do if I didant love you

Love From:

Above: A message I wrote when I got to Nigeria in 1980 but kept and gave it to my mum Kind when I returned in 1996.

Mum Kind brought out all my toys that she had kept for me. I was overwhelmed and couldn't believe I had been very much in their memories just as they were in mine. I took one look at the toys and burst out crying. They could not understand why tears were rolling down my cheeks. They thought the outburst was strange. I sat them all down and told them everything about my life and the adverse experiences I'd endured when I left them in 1980. By the end of it, they were crying harder than I was.

Amongst the toys were my favourite toys ever! I had the Fisher-Price face telephone that I pulled along, and my lovely family treehouse that formed into a tree ball. I would open and collapse it so many times that Dad couldn't understand how it never broke into pieces. I also had an orange and a brown monkey. My most favourite toys ever were a mother and baby tortoise. There was a string attached from the mother tortoise to the baby, and I would pull the rope. As the mother tortoise shuffled along, the rope would get shorter, playing the tune from the famous Coca-Cola advert 'I love to see…in perfect harmony'.

Mum also gave me all the letters that my classmates had sent me when I had chicken pox back in 1980. She had kept them safe for all those years. I got around twenty-eight letters from them. I still have them. Reading the letters truly put a smile on my face; they made me chuckle and brought back sweet memories. One also made me sob a little. It read:

Dear Bas
I hope you come back to school before you leave Ratby because we might not see you again.

The innocent words of a child are humbling. A few of them asked funny questions that only children can get away with:

I wonder what colour your chicken pox are. Are your chicken pox blue, red, orange, or yellow?

It took me years before I thought how badly my departure from my foster family affected them all. One of my foster sisters mentioned how she too was numb for days, not handling my departure well. Coming to terms with the fact that their little Bas would no longer be with them was difficult for everyone.

After reminiscing about the good old days, Mum insisted I took the toys with me to give to my kids when I decided to have them. I asked her to kindly donate them all to a children's hospice in Leicester instead. I felt I should give them to children who needed them more than I did and, since I hadn't had my children yet, it didn't feel right to hold onto them.

I was saddened to hear that Grandma and Grandpa in Torquay had passed away, but it was also comforting to know that they had lived a beautiful life with everybody around them. They were simply the best. They impacted my life in the first years that mattered most and, for that, I

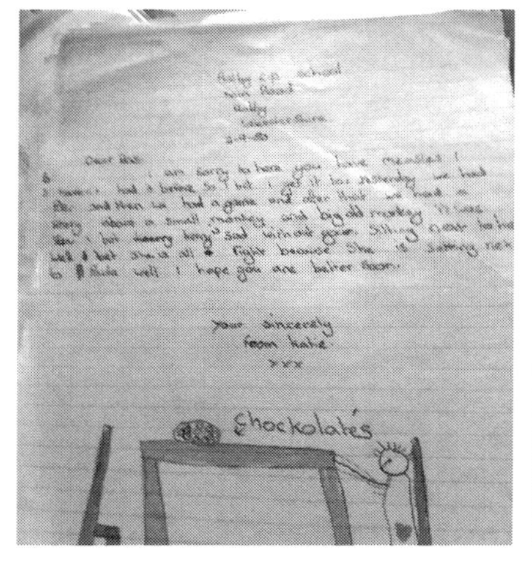

Dear Bas

your sincerely
from katie
xxx

Dear Bas

Yours Sincerely
Kerry

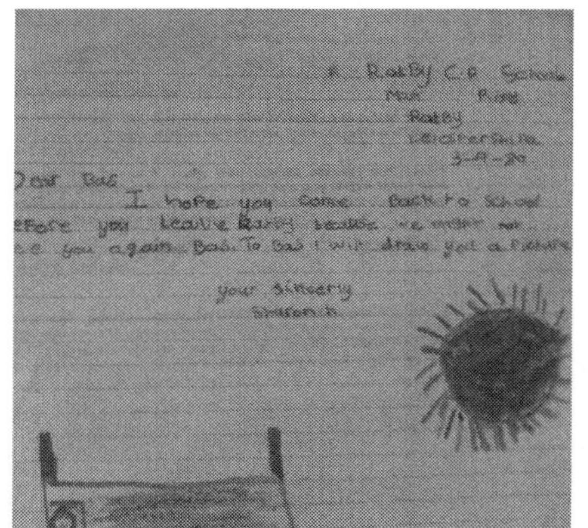

Ratby C.P School

Dear Bas
I hope you come back to school

your sincery
Sharon

Yours Sincerely
Joanne

Top left: A message from my classmate Katie, saying how much my best friend was missing me.

Top right: From my best friend Kerry.

Bottom left: From my classmate Sharon.

Bottom right: From my close friend Joanne.

am grateful. Mum told me how much everyone missed me, and, although they yearned to see me, they never knew whether they would see me again.

Reuniting with my foster family was exhilarating. They arranged a welcome home party, and I spent a whole week with them. It was soul-gratifying. I told them they had been the continuous rainbows in my clouds. They kept me going.

Before I returned to the UK, I'd never come to terms with leaving my foster family. Another part of me healed when I was back in their arms again after so long.

In July 1997, a year after I'd come to the UK, I went back to Nigeria to marry my sweetheart that I'd met while studying at the polytechnic in 1993. It was a month before my twenty-fifth birthday. After my adverse childhood experiences, and particularly the sexual abuse, I remember feeling uneasy when men complimented me. I always felt they only said I was pretty because they wanted to have a relationship with me; I was quite paranoid. My husband asked me out for about two years before I finally said yes. He had a nice and gentle attitude and I believed that he must be serious if he stuck around for two years. We had a lovely time whilst at the polytechnic and I would often stay over at his, even when I was meant to go home.

I had disassociated myself from all my adverse experiences so it wasn't a painful experience to go back to Nigeria to get married, particularly when all I had in my mind was to get married and be rid of past pain. Our wedding was a joyous occasion and although my dad paid for most of the celebrations, I thought it was the least he could do after all the suffering he had caused me.

I returned to the UK immediately after our wedding in July 1997 and my husband joined me in 1998. This was because I had to invite him over as my husband, since he was a Nigerian citizen. The process took one year from the time we applied till the time he joined me in the UK. Even though I thought I should apply to attend a university in the UK when I first arrived, I couldn't wait to get married, change my name, and make a fresh start.

We began trying to have a baby. I remember getting increasingly agitated when I didn't conceive. When I did get pregnant, I miscarried. I was devastated.

I carried on with my life, but still felt the need to write to my father. It was as if I couldn't get to grips with anything I laid my hands on until I unburdened the hurt and pain my dad had caused me.

On 19th September 1999, I wrote the longest letter I had ever written to my father. He replied. His response was nowhere near satisfactory, but it was satisfying at the time to know that I had gained some of my power back by being courageous enough to face him in that way.

It gave me some satisfaction that he acknowledged everything I had endured all those many years ago. I knew it had happened, but there were times when I dissociated myself so much that those memories were hard for me to comprehend.

I know some people can't write to their abuser(s), as some perpetrators might have passed away. I don't know what I would have done if I hadn't had the opportunity to write the letter and even get a response to it. I can say that writing and ripping up some notes that I didn't send also helped.

Not everyone who has undergone adverse childhood experiences can do this, and it's known to be dangerous to do this if the contents of the letter don't sit well with the perpetrator – if, for example, it states in the message that the perpetrator will be exposed. The contents of my letter were details of questioning 'why' and sharing with my dad how much hate I felt for him at the time.

I wrote several letters to him when my emotions ran high. I ripped them up afterwards as I wasn't bold enough yet to give them to him.

In 2004, my best friend Fisayo came to the UK. I told her why I had ended up in a fight with her all those years ago. I told her everything about my father. She felt terrible that she hadn't figured it all out when

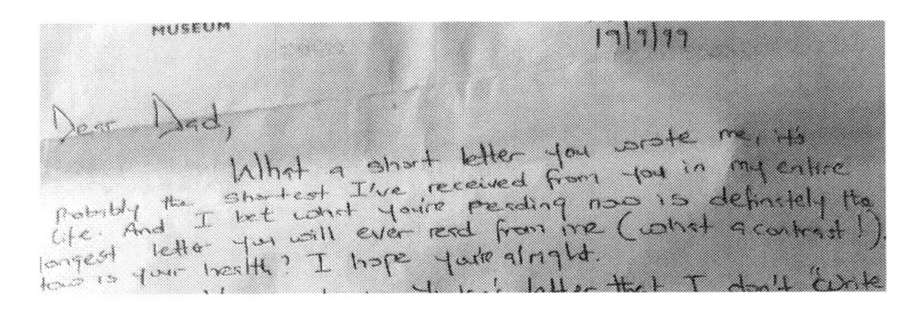

MUSEUM

17/7/97

Dear Dad,

What a short letter you wrote me, it's probably the shortest I've received from you in my entire life. And I bet what you're reading now is definitely the longest letter you will ever read from me (what a contrast!). How is your health? I hope you're alright.

Above: A snippet of the letter I wrote to my biological father.

we were in school. I said I hid my feelings, so there was no way she could get into that world of mine. I apologised unreservedly for my reaction. She totally understood and said it was OK; she wrapped her arms around me and we both became emotional.

I visited my foster family quite regularly and had the most fantastic news when I returned from a long weekend to Leicester for my foster brother's wedding in early February 2001. I conceived in February and gave birth to our gorgeous son in November. We went on to have our adorable daughter in 2005. Although I now had my own family, I didn't take time to look after myself. I was busy being busy. I was studying, working full time, and was being consumed by the past even though I didn't know I was.

I was often ashamed of telling people about my family dynamics but was always happy to talk about my foster family. I started to think about how I needed to stop being ashamed of my existence, but I wasn't intentional enough about doing that. I still held on deeply to my fondest memories in Ratby and always nurtured within me the kindness they had showed me. I heard a lot about fostering when I came back; it seemed strange to me that children got mistreated in foster homes. I became even more grateful for being with the Kind family. I looked back all through the years and confidently knew there was a reason I got placed with the 'Kind' family. It prepared me for some 'unkindness' in the world.

In 2006, when I was thirty-four years old, I learnt that my foster sister Carolyn had passed away. She left us when she was forty-three years old. When I got the phone call, I remember lowering myself to the floor and holding my head between my knees. I couldn't believe it. I was consumed by pain. I had gotten up early that morning, preparing to travel to Leicester to go to see her as I knew that she was losing her battle with cancer. I was determined to see her. Now I wouldn't have a chance. I've never stopped missing her. My heart always melts within me, knowing how loving she was to me, and how she gave me this sense of what having a big sister meant.

CHAPTER 14

Being Silenced

My childhood experiences, that led to trauma, were the reason I felt like a caged bird as I grew up. Although I enjoyed being around people and often had plenty to say, my insecurities would get there first; rushing my words, perhaps even making me say the wrong things. I unconsciously did anything that would stop me from reaching deep inside, from getting to my painful parts. I prevented anything from startling the caged bird that I suppressed, refusing to let it come out gracefully.

Several years back, everyone was at my house. I had all my siblings, my mum, my nephews and nieces over for a little lunch. It's always a unique and memorable experience, even if it meant that I'd woken up at 5 am to make all the arrangements necessary, ensuring everyone was happy.

While all our kids were busy playing upstairs, my mum, siblings and I gathered around the dining table, reminiscing about growing up in Nigeria. We were meeting my sister-in-law for the first time and were trying to embarrass my brother in the process.

We were talking about our mean uncles and aunties back in Nigeria, and the nice ones too. I remember attempting to say something, and felt an instant nudge in my side. It was my mum, and she asked if I could come to the kitchen with her for a minute.

'My dear,' she said when we were safely out of earshot. 'You don't need to get involved in the conversations when they start talking about uncles and aunties, you know what I mean?'

I paused and looked at her, a little bit puzzled, but I had an instinctive sense as to what she might mean. With a deep sigh, I simply replied, 'Hmmm, OK, Mum, no problem.'

She left the kitchen and I stood there, thinking to myself, *Have I just been asked to hush? Again? At my age?*

I shook my head in disbelief. I immediately felt different and ashamed. My mum thought it would be too complicated to explain that I had a different father to the rest of my five siblings. It's the norm not to speak of a child that was born out of wedlock. But I don't think we think of the implications of such 'hushes'.

She didn't mean anything malicious towards me. She didn't realise the effect of what she asked me to do, or not do. She simply wanted to avoid questions that might be awkward. Most of us might do something similar to this without processing the effects of our actions.

Silencing occurs in many ways for many reasons; each of us has his or her sea of unspoken words. English is full of overlapping terms. Silence is what allows people to suffer without recourse, which will enable hypocrisies and lies to grow and flourish, crimes to go unpunished. If our voices are essential aspects of our humanity, to be rendered voiceless is to be dehumanised or excluded from one's humanity.[1]

I had grown up feeling some level of shame and awkwardness now and again. I got reminded continuously in some way or another that I was different, no matter how hard I tried to fit in. I put on a façade to get by; lacking authenticity. For instance, when my half-siblings would talk about an uncle, their uncle from their dad, if an outsider was present I would nod and play along as if I knew who they were talking about, just so that I could fit in. I wouldn't ask any questions just so that I could blend in and not let the visitor know we had different fathers. Being ashamed had become so ingrained in me that I couldn't bring myself to speak about having a different father to my siblings.

I recall feeling another level of shame when I attended an aunt's seventieth birthday celebration a few years later. There were a lot of relatives present at the party, and I observed two men, possibly in their late sixties, who took a glance at me, then looked back at each other with an expression of shock on their faces. They walked up to me, and I greeted them in the usual Nigerian way, ignoring the fact that I had just seen them look at me with so much shock on their faces. I tried not to look as confused as I was.

One of them boldly said to the other, 'That is her, you know, Omo Leicester.' *The child from Leicester.* I knew what they meant. Ignoring their lack of manners, I introduced myself. They nodded and asked how I was. At that point, I felt the urge to be rude, but I held back. Even though I had beautiful attire on with a brightly coloured head tie, over the course of the party I felt ashamed as they mentioned it to more and more people, and I could feel their glances towards me. Going back home that day, I felt hurt and angry.

Over the years, I learnt never to be defined by what people thought of me. The fact that I was born out of wedlock means nothing about who I am. I gave them the power to make me feel bare and ashamed. I thought, never again! Once people label us, we get negated. Once people place a label on us, we must then become what they expect us to be; belittled and ashamed of our existence. The label on us can make us feel what people want us to feel. The phrase 'as we think, so shall we be' springs to mind. If we think that we should feel the shame of our very existence, then that is what we will become. If we pay attention to what other people expect from us, or what they say our limitations should be, that's what we will believe we should be. We can't focus on what we want, because what they wish for us to be will continue to manifest in us.

I had allowed those two men to place me into an 'identity crisis' box. I'd allowed their thoughts of me to weaken me.

Part of being, living and breathing authenticity means living by my standards of having no guilt. I decided not to live by the standards of others who wanted me silenced over things that would bring 'shame' to them.

Dancing our dance is what makes us unique. I am no accident. The fact that we are here matters, it's miraculous, and nothing about our lives is an accident. I learnt to stop limiting myself. Dancing my dance ensures that I don't live in a world where I seek to control it so that my fears don't get stimulated. I learnt not to go back to reach for a reason why I couldn't attain my goals.

There is freedom in feeling no shame. My confidence comes from knowing that there is something greater than me that taps me on my shoulder and keeps me going in a flow that aligns my personality with my soul.

I still got embarrassed and ashamed about my existence, to some degree, particularly when others reminded me of it. I knew there had to be another way.

When my kids were growing up, I rarely spoke to them about my family dynamics. They both thought I had the same father as my siblings from my mother's side. Due to the abuse I'd suffered at the hands of my father, as my kids got older, I distanced my children from him. It was easy to do this since he resides in Nigeria, and we are in the UK. Yet my son would sometimes ask why I rarely spoke about my father. I always felt a level of guilt because I would tell him that I didn't agree with the 'choices Grandpa made'. But I would also think that that statement was so incomplete that one day it could be used against me. I don't have to agree with other people's choices; that wasn't the reason. I always felt guilty for not being honest with my children.

My kids had gone to a social gathering, and when they got back, my son said, 'Mum, can I ask you something please?'

I said, 'Sure, go ahead, dear.'

He said, 'Are you and my uncles and aunt from a different father?'

I was surprised that he asked me and quickly asked where he'd heard that. He said a close relative had mentioned it to him. I was angry and thought it was not their place to mention anything to my children. I sat my son down and explained everything to him and vowed never to keep my existence a secret. I got distraught, thinking that the family member had done that out of spite because they knew I didn't want my children to know me and my siblings had different fathers, for two reasons. One was that as a middle child, it would be awkward to explain to my children; and secondly, I didn't want my children to know anything about my dad. I had, as a result of being ashamed on two levels, also silenced myself. From that day, I decided I would ensure, wherever possible, that everything my children heard about me would come from me first.

One of the biggest challenges to overcoming the things that have happened to us in the past is our culture. I believe this to be true for most of us. In the Nigerian culture, calling out someone within the family who has violated you in some way could be seen as bringing 'shame' to the family. It is mainly the case if the perpetrator is a respected person within the community. Just like in many other cultures, a sexual abuse survivor is expected to carry on and forget about the past. The victim will almost certainly be alienated from the family and seen to have brought 'shame' upon the family if they speak out. Never mind those who have inflicted the pain in the first place – it's a matter of, 'Let it go! That's all in the past now.' The reason why 'let it go' does not work is because we get told to lock up inside of us those parts of us that were most hurt when the abuse occurred in the first place. Silencing the victim is adding insult to injury.

Our viable natural state is loving, caring, confidence, calmness and so many other positive attributes that we have within us. These natural states were subsequently traumatised, forcing those positive attributes to hide. Humanity faces a new stark reality. We have a choice to evolve or live in the past.

Cultural norms often conflict with our self-worth in ways that attempt to silence us because of shame. Being ashamed of our childhood experiences imprints on us, limiting our belief in ourselves. I am grateful for all of me today, but I must heal, and for that reason, I will have to climb over the cultural beliefs of 'shame' that are in my way.

If we believe in Jesus or indeed know of his stories, we will see that he became the victim so we could stop victimising others or playing the victim ourselves. I thank Jesus for holding our shame and nakedness so fearlessly and so publicly, so I do not need to hide or deny our human reality. I no longer need to carry the guilt of what happened to me. Jesus already did that for me, so that I can be free.

As we evolve, culture will need to keep up with the modern world to survive and be sustainable in a knowledge-packed and spiritually enlightened world. If culture stagnates, it's undeniable that everything we strive to become diminishes because we have culture as our gatekeeper that stops us from reaching the most authentic and highest version of ourselves. It attempts to stop us from getting to higher ground to quench our thirst and to feed our hunger for freedom of expression.

CHAPTER 15

Reading To Healing

Understanding more about the connection between my mind, body and brain and how I could be more progressive in my healing journey was crucial to me. I also still bore resentment towards my father. I buried that side of me, and I was getting on with my life without letting myself think about it. I didn't know that the hurt and pain inside of me was manifesting in different areas of my life. I used to get worked up over little things. If my family and friends arrived late at my house when I invited them over for a dinner or small social gathering, I would get irritable and snappy. Even though my intentions were good and all I thought of was to make them all happy, I was angry over my family's lateness. An evening that should have been a lovely one that I had planned so well for would turn out to be a disaster. Arguments would ensue, and I would get even more irritable.

I tried to ensure that I always gave my children opportunities to express themselves. For many years, I worked in various roles at a charitable library organisation.I especially enjoyed being part of the reading campaign for schools. I visited my children's school to talk to them about the importance of having qualified librarians present. School libraries provide more than just books and other databases of accurate information and educational activities. They provide a haven for all students to think, create, share, grow and be expressive. I worked in that organisation for over sixteen years.

While I was working at the library organisation, and my children were in primary school, I was always keen to know what was going on in their school. I wanted to see the facial expressions of mine and other children to see if they were happy at school; this was important to me. I needed to be on the inside and so I got drawn into being a parent governor where I could, to an extent, have a say in the affairs of the school.

I always tried to think of innovative and creative ways of doing things with my children, their friends and my nephews and nieces. We often baked cookies and cakes, drew lots of pictures and did lots of painting. We read all kinds of books, like The *7 Habits of Happy Kids* by Sean Covey. And we told lots of stories. I regularly taught them different subjects such as Maths and Literacy; I continued to teach my kids and my nieces as they prepared to go to secondary school. While at my house in Essex, I recall asking my children and two of my friends' children to write a story about anything that came to them. My friend's daughter wrote the most touching and honest story I had ever read. Her expressions ran deep. I gave them around fifteen to twenty minutes to write the story. When she finished, she handed it to me with a sad-looking face. I asked her if she was OK, and she said, 'You'll know why when you read my story, Auntie.'

In the story, she expressed how she felt sad about her mum feeling lonely, and wrote about how her dad used to mistreat her mum. It brought tears to my eyes. I pulled her to one side and asked if she wanted to talk about her story; she said she would love to. We spoke at length and I gave her a hug. Although I was aware of everything she had written because her mum had confided in me, I was shocked that she detailed it in the way she did. I rang her mum and explained what I'd read. She had no idea that her daughter felt that way and was grateful that we'd done such an exercise. Being fully expressive is undoubtedly healing in its own right, and I pray that we are all guided in ways that make us understand the meaning of being able to own our voice.

As a governor at my children's school, I became part of a team that looked after a scheme called 'A life in the year of'. Part of this scheme entailed the children in different year groups reading to parents. A parent would sit in the class for the whole day to witness what went on. The children were around the ages of eight and nine and it was lovely to see how much fun they had. I saw myself through them and how I was at their age; a bubbly and expressive child. I'd get absorbed in how they read a variety of books, ranging from *Private Peaceful* by Michael Morpurgo and *Matilda* by Roald Dahl to *A Series of Unfortunate Events* by Lemony Snicket. I'd listen to how expressive many of them were in their storytelling.

As a governor, over the years, I got to know my community quite well and would often say hello to teachers, parents and children as I walked by the school on the way to work. I became more interested in reading about childhood experiences and spirituality.

I recall a close family member making reference to the fact that she expected me to have been a lot higher in my career than I currently was. I believed I should have had more career progression too. I justified my slow advance by the fact that I had a lot of physical ailments, and that I frequently got admitted to hospital. It was easier to stay in the organisation that was used to me being out of work for more than two months at a time. And, of course, I blamed my father and gave him my power. I lacked confidence, even though I appeared to be confident outwardly.

I started a journey of discovering myself. I read a variety of positive-thinking self-help books. I loved reading, so it came naturally to me. I'd stopped reading in my secondary school days when my attention was more on just wanting to be safe. I dipped in and out of reading books, but I knew I still loved reading. I can't even remember how I got back into reading, I just did. One of the first books I recall reading in my late twenties to early thirties was Stephen Covey's *The 7 Habits of Highly Effective People*. There were a lot of golden nuggets in the book; the one problem I found was when I read parts about 'depositing into people's emotional bank account'. This was along the lines of reconciling our differences or making amends. I struggled because I hadn't begun a journey of deep healing yet. I needed to deposit into my 'inner-feeling bank account' first, so I failed miserably at trying to be happy with everyone else or accept their apologies when they had hurt me.

I found that I got taken for granted even more, which led me to be irritable and explosive in my reactions. I was applying the readings with an attitude of 'I need to be liked by everyone'. That was, of course, the wrong way and not what the author, Covey, intended his book to convey. The one most important single message I did get from the book and use today is 'Beginning with the End in Mind'. That sat well with me.

I then stumbled into spiritual readings. They became my light bulb moments. They were the books I needed before fully applying Covey's concepts. The spiritual readings gave more meaning to my religious beliefs that I had struggled with in my teen years and as a young adult.

Once I'd eased myself into reading a lot more, I realised that so many spiritual teachings in the books resonated with me. I learnt to recognise the rage I had, and that I had a 'pain body'. I started to learn how not to identify with the attributes that I had acquired over the years as a result of my adverse childhood experiences. I began to deal with the root cause and be intentional about my healing journey.

I first came across the term 'pain body' around 2014 when I listened to Oprah interviewing Eckhart Tolle. He was one of my first virtual spiritual teachers, and I am so grateful for his teachings. I did have to listen several times before I could fully grasp his message because it was a higher type of reasoning. I wasn't used to that high level. I'd focused on religion and not spirituality in the past, so it was an entirely new concept to me. In Tolle's book *The Power of Now*, he explains that for as long as we are unable to access the present moment, every emotional pain is lodged in our body and mind. He goes on to say that this includes the pain suffered as a child. I remember thinking this resonated with me to a tee. Although the childhood experiences I'd endured had stopped when I was around fifteen or sixteen years old, I'd been consumed by hate and anger, and that part of me always referred to the past by manifesting itself in different forms. That was the case when I got angry with my best friend for calling me a 'daddy's girl'.

The problem I had was that I hadn't dealt with my feelings at that point because I didn't know how to. If I'm honest, I didn't think I had a problem. I just knew I was hurting badly. The earlier experiences of leaving my foster family and then leaving my half-siblings all contributed to my adverse childhood and traumatic events. My pain body continued throughout my adult life. I didn't realise that I was exhibiting my inner feelings. Those around me knew that there were times when I was erratic in my behaviour. As my children got older, particularly my daughter, I noticed that I was overly protective of her, even when there was no apparent danger or threat to her. Others would say I was paranoid. Her dad doted on her and is the most loving father to both of our children. He would never hurt them. I remember always saying that I would bathe her or dress her when she was a baby or a toddler. My inability to trust often caused friction between us. I had to learn to relax a bit more and be more trusting.

I was extremely thorough in all my dealings with both my children. At my children's nursery, I used a red book for both of my kids. I'd record everything that my kids had got up to the night before. I'd record if they'd had a cold, what they ate, what their habits were and all sorts. When mothers and fathers queued up in the morning to speak to the nursery manager before they dropped their kids off and dashed to work, I simply handed over my red book. I knew they'd never remember everything every parent said in the morning. In the evening, I would pick up the kids, and the nursery assistant would have written in the book what my kids got up to. We had a system going, although sometimes they thought I was a little on the crazy side, I'm sure.

I knew my childhood experiences must impact on those close to me in one way or the other. My perfectionist attitude was insane sometimes. I drove my kids mad with my expectations of their performance at school.

I remember my son coming home from school one day, saying there were messages written on a sheet of paper on the teacher's table. For some reason, the teacher had written the name of a student's parent beside each attribute they thought best described each parent. Some read, for example, Mrs Abraham – complains about lack of communication; Mr Smith – often angry; and then when it came to the message written about me, it read, Mrs Okunuga – too pushy. I remember justifying this term to my son, saying sometimes you have to strive to get what you want. I knew I did occasionally try to push through changes in the school, such as when I made forceful suggestions about children's welfare. An example was when I suggested the vital importance of a close connection between the school and social services if a child seemed unhappy. This was, of course, the usual protocol taken, but I would be driven by my pain and not able to express my opinions in an objective manner to effect the change I wanted to see. I would suggest some processes that were not within the school's budget and get irritable if it couldn't be implemented. These suggested processes could be, for instance, to call every student and find out how they were feeling or for someone to be appointed specifically to carry out some type of wellbeing task.The more I immersed myself in reading literature and spiritual books, the more I started to become calm and began to develop deliberate ways to respond to situations.

CHAPTER 16

Helping You Help Us

The benefits of meditating were becoming a revelation to me. I saw that it could make me calmer and improve my overall health and well-being. I hoped that by meditating I would be able to pass positive and loving energy to those around me. It was during one of the Bodybalance (a combination of Pilates, Tai chi and Yoga) classes that I discovered something I had been doing that I hadn't realised wasn't something everyone else did. For as long as I could recall, I'd always clenched my jaw. I hadn't realised that not everyone did this until my late thirties.

'Relax your jaws, open your mouths,' the teacher said, gently opening her mouth and rotating her neck. 'Stress and anxiety might make you constantly clench your jaw.'

I remember stopping all of a sudden. I opened my eyes to see what everyone was doing. They all seemed familiar with the teacher's instruction and not surprised as I was.

It was only then that I started the healing of releasing my clenched jaw. I still work on this, putting the letters 'CJ' on places easily visible to me, like my phone and PC. When I see them, I release my jaw if I had it clenched.

Although I was adopting some of the teachings, like meditating and going to Body Balance classes, I wasn't losing weight, nor was I feeling fulfilled in some of my present life experiences. I still suffered from the earaches that I'd had as a child well into my late thirties. I went to see the doctor once or twice, but when I didn't get any satisfactory answer, I started researching the different reasons for tinnitus. Although it's not proven that stress causes tinnitus, there are some suggestions that stressful situations are a contributing factor. It's also common for existing tinnitus to become worse during periods of high stress. For some people, tinnitus acts as their 'barometer' of stress, often worsening when difficult things are going on in life[1].

It was almost inevitable that my earache had everything to do with the childhood experiences I'd endured. I developed other physical ailments when I was around twenty-eight years old. I began to suffer from rheumatoid arthritis, an autoimmune disease where the immune system attacks parts of the body, especially the joints. The arthritis intensified when I put on more weight.

Although rheumatoid arthritis can be due to many factors such as hereditary traits, after thorough research, I concluded that it was as a result of my frequent stressful experiences as a child that led me to have physical ailments as an adult. The more frequently and severely a child is mistreated growing up, the more likely he or she is to develop arthritis by adulthood, according to new findings.[2] Psychological trauma, such as after childhood sexual abuse (CSA), has long-term physical consequences because stressful early life experiences cause immune dysregulation across the lifespan.[3]

Around 2014, I had a surgical procedure to remove a chronic ovarian cyst that had grown bigger and was on the verge of rupturing. It caused me to have excruciating pain. I was not aware of the correlation between the operation I had and the traumatic experiences I'd endured as a child and teenager. But when I woke up from the procedure, the doctor came to me looking puzzled.

He first put my mind at rest by saying, 'Mrs Okunuga, the procedure was successful.' He then went on to say, 'It was a difficult one. The procedure to remove the cysts you had is not uncommon, but you had unusually big cysts and chronic adhesions. The operation lasted well over four hours. It usually takes around two hours.'

The doctor said I had a lot of abdominal adhesions. Adhesions are areas of scar tissue that can cause organs or tissues in the abdomen to stick together. They are usually found in the small intestine where it loops and piles up. Adhesions can cause some of these loops to stick together, which can result in abdominal pain.

I started to wonder why I was having significantly more physical ailments than all of my siblings. I started researching all the disorders I had. I thought it was because I was the only one who had no other full biological sibling, and it could all be hereditary traits from both my parents that only I had.

During my studies at university, I often wandered off on the internet, searching for all kinds of information. I started to find close correlations between physical ailments in adulthood and childhood experiences. From 2017, I began to do more thorough research.

When something scary happens, stress hormones set your heart racing and make you break into a cold sweat. But if those hormones stay elevated for a long time, they can cause inflammation in the body and lead to lasting health problems.[4]

The Adverse Childhood Experiences (ACEs) I endured were close together. The ACEs could have caused my hormones to stay elevated for too long a period, leading to inflammation in my body.

Many physical consequences of child sexual abuse are known. These include widespread and chronic pain, sleeping problems, adult-onset arthritis, fibromyalgia, long-term fatigue, diabetes and circulatory, digestive, respiratory and musculoskeletal issues, as well as reproductive and neurological ones. Survivors often develop medically unexplained symptoms which go hand in hand with significantly higher healthcare use, such as a more significant number of visits to the emergency department, hospital outpatient department, pharmacy, primary care and specialty care than those without a CSA experience.[5]

The lack of retentive memory that caused some of my difficulties at school could have been what is known as 'brain fog'. This is the inability to have a sharp memory or a sharp focus. One of the most common causes of brain fog is just not sleeping enough.[6] I know this to be true for me. I stopped sleeping well from a very early age, around eight. My sleep deprivation, of course, got worse from when I turned twelve. There were nights when I only had about two or three hours of sleep. I was always on guard in case someone came into my room at night, so I needed to stay alert. It was worse at home, but also affected me in the dormitory at school. I also became a very light sleeper. I woke up at the slightest noise. As my dormitory had over forty girls in the rooms, there was always something that kept me awake.

It would be of great importance to health practitioners to know our personal story. Our stories will help them get to grips with patients that have repetitive physical ailments, resulting in several trips to the hospital or health clinics. Survivors of adverse childhood experiences will undoubtedly help health practitioners to understand some unexplained illnesses survivors have that experts have often never fully understood. The more we share our stories, the more there will be robust treatments. The more stories that get out in the open, the more sexual child abuse survivors can help practitioners help survivors.

Being the neatest girl in my secondary school days was admirable at the time. I took great pride in going up to the Commandant in front of the entire school during the assembly. I saw this as a positive attribute. But when I returned to the UK, I heard the term OCD several times and decided to look further into it. I was sure I had Obsessive Compulsion for cleanliness as a result of my childhood experiences.

When I came across the term OCD – a tendency to have excessive orderliness, perfectionism, and great attention to detail – I immediately thought about all my obsessive cleanliness and orderliness at school. My locker was always neat, and nothing was out of place. I'd rather be late leaving the dormitory than not straighten my bed over and over again before I went to class. OCD was me right there – that was one of my sub-personality traits. I thought, *Wow! That's what I had, and I got rewarded for it?* If there had been better pastoral care at the school, they could have made a connection between my behaviour and the reasons why I was exhibiting those characteristics.

I recall so many occasions in school and even as an adult where I'd clean excessively to exhaustion. When I was in secondary school, I would straighten my bed even as my friends sat on it. I cleaned my dormitory corner while people were standing there, and my friends had no idea, as I didn't at the time, that I was reacting from my 'hurting body'; the body and mind that kept telling me I was unclean and that everything had to be cleaner than clean. As an adult, I knew it had to stop because not only was it driving people away from me, it was too exhausting. Apart from wanting a clean house, I also cleaned so that people who came to my house would not judge me for seeing one thing out of place.

My perfectionist attitude almost certainly drove some family members away from me. They'd come visiting from Nigeria to spend the holiday in our house during the summer break. They saw my irritations first hand! I would get agitated with the whole family, clean all the time, and even though I loved their company and loved being around people, my desire got focused on having a spotless and squeaky-clean house.

Even though I had acknowledged to a great extent that I exhibited OCD traits, I refused to accept that it was something I could let go. I saw OCD as a mental disorder that couldn't be what I had when I read about other people's traits. I refused to think that I had some kind of cleanliness 'illness'. Even though the definition pointed to specific attributes I had, I was in denial.

My inability to accept that I had compulsive traits all changed when I had a wakeup call in 2016. My pyrrhic victory – keeping my house spotless, doing other tasks at the cost of looking after myself – had to come to an end. I was trying to be Cinderella, cooking, cleaning and baking all sorts until I dropped, while ignoring my weaknesses and not taking proper care of myself.

I'd had a yearly GTT (Glucose Tolerance Test) for the past four years. The GTT was as a result of having gestational diabetes during both my pregnancies. I was almost sure to become diabetic later in life as a result.

Women who experienced childhood trauma have a higher risk of gestational diabetes because they develop depressive symptoms in adulthood, not because they have a poorer lifestyle.[7]

I was due for my GTT review. My doctor sat me down and opened up my notes. I listened to him say, 'Toyin, I'm afraid the next time you come for your appointment in six months, you will have diabetes.'

As I looked him in the eyes, I shook my head gently but confidently and said, 'I won't, sir.'

I thought, *You can't get bolder than that, Toyin. No pressure!*

On the way home, as I drove, I said aloud, 'Toyin, you've got to convert that energy into looking after you! You have to define how you want to be because it's within your control to do so. Remember all the teachings of

Above: Me, before I lost weight, and me five months later.

Eckhart Tolle: 'Break out of the old pattern of present-moment denial and present-moment resistance. Make it your practice to withdraw attention from the past and future when they're not needed.'

If I stood a chance of reversing what my doctor had just said to me, I needed to be deliberate in my actions. I knew I was in control at that point as to whether or not I would become diabetic. At fourteen stone and only 5 ft 4 inches tall, I was obese. I focused on setting attainable goals and being accountable for what I ate and drank. I became more intentional about my day-to-day life and exercised regularly. When I went back to my doctor, I had no traces of diabetes. I had lost four stone in five months.

Once I lost the weight, I felt much more confident. It was very satisfying that I could accomplish this and stay on track for over four years. Losing the weight gave me that confidence to feel unstoppable in anything I wanted to achieve.

CHAPTER 17

Becoming One With Self

In 2018, when I was in my mid-forties, I completed my Business Management degree at the Open University. The flexibility of this university fitted my lifestyle perfectly, primarily because it allowed me time to look after the kids and, once I finished, I worked in public and banking industries for just under two years.

While I was studying, I felt a real sense of accomplishment, and though I finished when I was in my mid-forties, I was another step closer to my healing journey. I had battled with inner pain for so long. I was proud of my achievement, but I knew I still had more work to do.

When studying Maslow's Hierarchy of Needs[1] during my degree programme, I remember looking at the triangle. From the bottom, I read upwards as the triangle narrowed towards the top, and I started to see where I was. I began to tick each need in order, one by one. When I got to 'Esteem needs: prestige and feeling of accomplishment', I thought, *Hmmm, what is it to feel accomplished?* I was full of gratitude that I had finally moved up the ladder from a 'sense of belonging'. I had sat there for so long. I had now finished my degree and could tick the fourth stage, the penultimate level.

It was as though Maslow was standing in front of me with his arms folded and saying, 'Hey, Toyin, you've got one more ladder to climb. Remember your passion, what you want to stand for – self-actualisation?' Self-actualisation was what I needed, through achieving all that I know I can, to my full potential. My voice, that voice that was silenced and that I was scared to let loose all these years. I'd got the job with the company I'd always wanted. I was grateful. I knew it was time for me to use my voice.

I've learnt to feel the emotion and let it go. I still feel my feelings, but the strength is in how I respond to them. Even though being taken from my foster family as an eight-year-old was one of the most hurtful times in my life, I know my parents took the decision that they thought was the best one. Looking back, I believe it was the right thing to do. I know for sure that I am far from being that 'perfect parent'. I know my past will have affected my parenting syle; even though I can't place a finger on anything specifically – possibly many! My kids, no doubt, will have plenty to say! The one thing I do know for sure is how protective I am of them. I have in recent years started to develop different types of empowering 'muscles' and leave everything to God, because I don't have the power to protect them against all harm. I pray, strive to bring them up with best intentions and let my deliberate actions of working to be the best I can be do the rest.

Over the years, I found out that my foster parents had pleaded with my birth parents to leave me with them and proceed to go to Nigeria with my other birth siblings. If they had left me in the UK, I could have had a feeling of neglect, even though at the time, I wouldn't have seen it that way.

I might not fully have known my identity as a black woman if I had stayed in a predominantly white area with a white family in the UK. Neither would I have fully understood the culture of my birth parents, nor had the opportunity to experience village life; paddling about in the beautiful flowing streams of fresh water. I'm grateful that I've had the opportunity to know the native heritage of my biological family. I'm thankful that I had the incredible experience of learning how to cook Nigeria's most delicious traditional dishes. I enjoy teaching my children how to cook traditional meals today. I appreciate wearing the most beautiful-coloured traditionally sewn outfits like laces and ankara prints. I wear them with pride.

Top: On my graduation day.
Bottom left and right: Me wearing traditional outfits.

Varied life experiences enlighten us. They enrich our thinking ability and teach us to appreciate lives lived in different parts of the world. I feel incredibly fortunate that I had the best of both worlds in terms of having the most significant and most crucial early years of my childhood spent with my most beautiful foster family. I also have an excellent extended family and friendship connections. I enjoy those relationships today.

Over the years, I've found it quite healing when I look at the holistic picture and look through the lens of my mum and stepdad and their decision to make the move they did. I don't get bitter. When I found out that we were all taken to Nigeria because it was time for us to go to see our grandparents as they were getting older and getting desperate to see their grandchildren, I empathised with my parents and understood why they did what they did. They did what they thought was best with the awareness and knowledge they had at the time.

When I was coming to terms with my childhood experiences, I informed all my siblings and close relatives of the abuse I'd endured at the hands of my father. They were horrified and stunned, but it was quite clear that I was expected to put it all in the past and move on with my life. It was perceived that I was bringing up what I should now have forgotten. This expectation is not uncommon in Nigerian culture; it is the case in a lot of other cultures that I've come across, like the Asian community. It is considered to be shameful if you expose those who have wronged you in that way.

Tempora mutantur, et nos mutantamur in illis. This Latin phrase is interpreted as: 'Times are changed, we also are changed with them'. When I started my healing journey, I hoped that the passage of time would make shame no longer rule our lives. I was hopeful that the advancement of technology would intertwine with cultural beliefs. I am still confident that we will remove the veil of shame and make it easier to climb over roadblocks and gain a deep sense of peace within. Traumatic events, unfortunately, do not suddenly disappear, nor do we fully heal because of the passage of time. Even when we do work on ourselves, I truly believe that although we progress in our healing journey, we do not fully heal those parts that are hurt deeply within us. I hold firm to my faith as a Christian and spiritual being. I know that God continues to renew my strength and I am grateful for my journey of sustained and progressive healing.

I first came across the concept of 'parts' during my healing journey in 2018, when I read *The Body Keeps the Score* by Bessel van der Kolk. This book was the single most crucial piece of writing that solidified all my previous knowledge and understanding of my childhood experiences. It highlighted clearly how my childhood experiences had impacted my life choices and behaviour as an adult. The book has a lot of significant cases that resonated with my childhood experiences. The one aspect that I took further was the discovery of 'Self'. Van der Kolk explained this concept in depth, stating that 'the Self is like an orchestra conductor who helps all the parts to function harmoniously as a symphony rather than a cacophony'. The term 'cacophony' here stood out to me so well, and I could see my different personalities as a mixture of disorganised parts of a whole me. Although I was kind, compassionate, loving and caring, I also had intense irritability, anger and pain. All these manifested in me when, for instance, I sensed harm towards a child, or if I felt that someone wanted to take advantage of my kindness towards them. When I got agitated, it was a part of my inner Self talking, but this part was the one that got forced out of its normal state. It was traumatised. It was apparent that it wasn't the incident that was happening in the present moment that was enraging me. It was something deeper I had experienced that externalised in a way that caused me not to be measured in my approach.

A light bulb moment for me was when Bessel van der Kolk referred to the Internal Family Systems model (IFS). It spoke to my childhood experiences and how they linked to my behaviour from my teenage years to my adulthood. I decided to research further into the IFS model. The IFS model is an integrative approach to individual psychotherapy developed by Richard C. Schwartz in the 1980s. He explained how the 'Self' knows how to heal, allowing us to become integrated and whole.[2]

I was eased into IFS because I had initially read *The Body Keeps the Score*. The IFS model also consolidated my previous understanding of Eckhart Tolle's *The Power of Now* and the concept of the 'pain body'.

I followed a lot of the mindfulness-based exercises on Schwartz's online videos, and they made me understand an aspect of myself that I could never truly reconcile before. The IFS model showed me that we all have different parts that make us up as a whole. We all start with loving parts when we are born, and these good parts get forced into destructive features, and some into extreme beliefs, by traumas that have impacted us throughout our childhood.

From a practical person's perspective, at first it appeared to have a kind of unearthly or supernatural strangeness to it. But as I practised my daily routine of reading my bible, meditation and breathing; and read my regular spiritual books such as *Change your Thoughts – Change your Life* by Dr Wayne Dyer and *The Seat of the Soul* by Gary Zukav, the IFS model began to tie in nicely with my beliefs.

From my experience, I knew that I'd carried a burden of shame for so long, and I internalised my feelings. I also accepted it when people told me that I had always been too sensitive and couldn't change that about myself. A few family members and some of my close friends, in particular, often made these statements and I believed them too. I identified with them. I knew IFS was indeed what I needed. From the model, I now know that my 'Self' is at the heart of all positive attributes like courage and creativity. Something further inside of me had been traumatised.

My healing was more profound from that time on. I do sometimes drift back and forth. I'm a work in progress for sure. I know my understanding of the Bible teachings are a lot deeper and more meaningful to me. I combine my Bible teachings with other knowledge- packed resources. I haven't followed the entire IFS teachings, but my understanding of it is comforting. It satisfies me to know that it is utterly OK when we dissociate ourselves from adverse experiences to carry out daily tasks. I now know that our Self – the complete and whole of us – has all kind attributes. I now understand why my ability to feel no shame but to operate from a higher level of compassion and empathy towards others is due to my Self-leadership. Schwartz calls these the eight Cs – courage, connectedness, curiosity, confidence, calmness, creativity, clarity and compassion.[3]

I realised I was on a path to therapeutic healing when I could tick every one of these eight Cs, which Schwartz explained are present when emotional healing is happening. Of the eight Cs, I feel a strong sense of 'connectedness' – an intuitive understanding that the suffering of others affects me because of my connectedness to them. I also know this to be true, as I feel no 'shame' in sharing my experiences. I don't feel ashamed because the connection I perceive is as a result of a link to a meaningful purpose or a higher calling above the circumstances of my daily life activities.

My healing process became even more of a necessity when I read a lot of literature around intergenerational trauma, or what Schwartz calls 'legacy burdens'. These are powerful organisers of our minds and behaviours. They are the beliefs and emotions we absorb from family, peers, ethnic groups and cultural contexts regarding ourselves and/or groups with whom we identify, as well as groups we consider 'other'.[4]

I was determined to go through the full healing process and work on any reversible damage I might have unconsciously passed on to my children. I recognise how my own experience has resulted in me being hushed and controlled. Both my parents had unreconciled, unfortunate childhood or adult experiences. I inherited my parents' injury, unconsciously. In rising above the remnants of my parents' trauma (known or unknown to them), I help to heal future generations.

Gary Zukav, the author of *The Seat of the Soul*, a number-one New York Times bestseller, explained how people who are hurting operate from the angle of 'external power'. That power is outward, the kind of energy that gives them happiness but not joy. It's the kind of power a boss exercises when they sack a worker because they have the power to do and undo. The teachings of 'external power' consolidated my understanding of my other spiritual teachers. I began to understand that when he abused me, my dad was exercising external power. I started to believe that one single act did not define him in totality (although I know sometimes it's hard to find one good thing about a person who is mostly known for their evil-doing). For me not to bury this aspect of un-forgiveness, I knew I had to deal with it. I had to think that his act of unkindness towards me was one aspect of him. It was one part of his 'sub-personality'. I learnt to see that my dad, like me, had a 'splintered Self' that needed healing. It gave me more reason to empathise, although I didn't know what was 'splintered' in his 'Self'. It was inevitable that every discrepancy between his conscious intention and the emotions that accompanied it pointed directly to a splintered aspect of his 'Self' that required healing.[5]

I learnt that love liberates us, and forgiveness is inherently part of that. Once we begin to realise that we have a limited time on earth, we recognise the need to live abundantly, seeing that what affects that abused little child affects us all and cannot be separated from us if we want to see growth and happiness in the world.

Above: Me, during one of my meditation sessions.

CHAPTER 18

Hush To Roar

When I read Michelle Obama's *Becoming* in December 2018, it was the golden nugget I needed. It was like I needed permission to go out into the world. The one message I kept in my head, even memorising the page number in the book, was when she made reference to the power of using our voice. I remember first reading the message and thinking, *But I suppose that might be for those who don't have my twisted adverse childhood journeys*, and then I thought, *Nope! Everything that has happened to me has already happened to someone else.* I felt validated that I would be doing the right thing by using my voice. It sat well with me.

My childhood experiences shaped my life as an adult, and I would often get angry about how I got silenced about all of my unfortunate life experiences. I knew I loved talking and I often did, but not in a way that would bring out my brilliance sometimes. I'd hide that part of me, unintentionally. Yet I could see that continuing down the path of not communicating fully would lead me to be that pressure cooker for ever – just waiting to lash out. I knew I had everything I needed to reach inside me. There is so much of me to give, to give lovingly, but that wasn't transcending outwardly. Not fully.

The feeling of being different, different from my siblings because of my family dynamics, was eating me up. I was slowly giving way to the inner voice that would say, 'Hush, no one should ever know the authentic you, you're a secret.'

I knew I needed to invest in myself. Having my degree was great. I remember contemplating studying for a Master's degree and then possibly a doctorate because I knew I had it in me to achieve such attainments. I always believed I would have had those achievements if it wasn't for my experiences. Yet I knew it wasn't what I needed to fulfil my purpose. I knew that the experiences I'd endured required more internal healing, not so much what the educational system offered. I needed to reach for the voice that I'd hidden for so long. I needed personal growth and healing in communication to release the inner child. Only then could I be genuinely authentic.

I invested a lot in my personal growth to reach for my 'roar', to get my voice that was measured, not rushed or agitated. It was important that I enrolled in a course with someone who was spiritual and believed in a higher power and was authentic. Although I was standing on top of my story and no longer 'swimming in it', I knew I had to tell my two teenage children. It was one of the hardest decisions I had to make. I was conscious that it wasn't for selfish reasons that I was making this decision. I didn't want to be free of my trauma by telling them and, as a result, burden them with the very thing that I had, the trauma. Yet I felt it was the right thing for me to do. I read lots and lots of cases about whether or not the very thing, trauma, that I was trying to get healed of was the same trauma that both my kids would get if I mentioned it to them. I prayed and sought a higher intervention on how to go about it. I got the wisdom and clarity I needed.

I said in the morning on that day that I would like to tell them something later that evening. When it was time, we sat down, and I started slowly. I eased them in by saying that I was sorry for not telling them that I had a different father from my half-siblings all those many years ago. I said it was regrettable that they had to hear it from someone else. I knew they were of an era where they see a lot more than I did when I was at their age. Technological awareness has made it easy for our children to be more enlightened than we can ever imagine. It felt right to tell both of them, and I was confident that with the proper communication, they would not get traumatised. I used the appropriate language for their teenage years. It was the most trauma-releasing experience I had ever felt.

I watched them both as I told them the experience. They had their eyes fixed on me. When I finished, they both got up and hugged me. It was the most extended and most prolonged hug I had ever got from them both. They said, 'Mum, you are so inspiring. We are proud of you.'

That was the greatest, most reassuring thing that had ever happened. I could now breathe, knowing that because of my deliberate and intentional communication with my children, they would be just fine.

I recall reading about trauma-informed care, an approach that has been introduced in Scotland, and that I hope will be adapted in all other areas and other countries too. In response to adverse childhood experiences, the model moves away from asking, 'What is wrong with you?' to asking, 'What has happened to you?' This question is fundamental to trauma-informed care[1].

With this new trauma-informed care, I hope that the question 'What happened to you?' might provide health professionals with a holistic view of what care patients need, given their experience as a child or young adult. I firmly believe that when everyone in a family setting is aware of what trauma another family member might have experienced, it will lessen, by using utmost care and communication, the chances of it becoming generational.

Learning a lot about trauma-informed care made me not be so hard on myself. I don't make excuses for my actions, but I now have a better understanding of the discovery of me. I now know that there is a direct correlation between our mind, body and brain. I am more enlightened about the fact that biological changes in a child have a direct correlation with physical and mental health experienced later in life as an adult. As a parent, I continue to be mindful of the fact that an event that might not seem traumatic to me can be traumatic to children. I also know that events like the death of a family member or a divorce can traumatise a child if there is no effective communication around such events.

Often, healing might come at a cost; there is an amount of risk that is always inseparable from healing. It can stir up emotions. I recall two incidences that took me back to the abuse I'd endured. I was part of a WhatsApp forum for my secondary school year, Set '91. It was 6th August 2019. My classmates were discussing their experiences back in Command School. Someone mentioned how he used to go to various places outside the school when we were on half-term. Suddenly someone posted another message, saying how he enjoyed staying at the Tati Hotel. I became breathless. I had not spoken about that place for over twenty years. It was a place I wanted to erase from my memory permanently. If ever scientists discover how to permanently erase past painful events, I will be first in line to get this out of my head.

What was said so innocently and had others talking about this lovely hotel made me breathless. I didn't know it would have such an impact on me. Through my daily meditation, being still with myself, through prayers and reading my Bible, it has become a lot easier to deal with and my spiritual teachers continuously remind me that the 'past has no power in the present moment'. Reaching deep inside of me through meditation has been a revelation around healing.

The other occasion was when a new member of the WhatsApp group couldn't remember who I was. A close friend of mine tried to trigger his memory by saying, 'You must remember Toyin. She was always awarded prizes for being the neatest girl in the school.' Although this didn't give me the same emotional feeling as the previous one, it made me think about how I could use my experience to help professionals recognise the possible signs of survivors of child sexual abuse.

We often have no idea that the adverse childhood experiences we have endured are responsible for our behaviours as adults. Enrolling on Lisa Nichols' communication programme revealed to me the effectiveness of my voice and how I needed to reach deep inside of me to heal. Lisa Nichols is an American, one of the world's most sought-out transformational speakers. She is CEO of Motivating the Masses.[2]

Enrolling with Lisa was an incredible experience, and it proved that having a university or college degree is not sufficient to grow if there are deep-rooted feelings that lie within us, particularly those areas that lead to trauma in our adult life.

In 2019 I enrolled in the course, which explores different communication strategies that allowed me to own my voice by mastering communication at a whole new level. I could relate to a lot of Lisa's struggles, especially how she communicated her understanding of always wanting to please everyone. She also mentioned how she had got stuck in a place of low self-worth. It all struck a chord with me. Being ready and willing to walk alone spoke volumes to me. The programme allowed me to realise how thirsty I was to get to my self-actualisation level. I followed this programme, and it allowed me to be more deliberate and intentional about ways of living my primary purpose. It made me realise how much I had it in me to take risks, such as unveiling shame for me to heal from my adverse childhood experiences. I was able to talk about my story in a safe environment to impact others.

Communicating in public spaces has been helping me to heal. It allows me to reach for the child within me, and that transcends into joy externally to others by making me calmer and confident.

To start healing from childhood traumas, I have found that it is vital that we free ourselves from the state of silence, moving from the pressure cooker explosive moments into teapot ones, gently releasing the steam, unlocking the inner child, slowly and gracefully.

Since attending Lisa's communication programmes, I have delivered speeches in corporate settings and public workshops to over seventy people without getting uneasy. I've owned the stage, and it has been incredible. Before I enrolled in Lisa's programme I used to feel everyone could see right through me when I spoke during my workplace presentations. It was like I was revealing to them everything about my childhood without saying anything about it. I immediately became conscious of how I thought I was perceived, rather than focusing on the delivery of my speech. I placed all the attention on me rather than my audience.

During one of my presentations, before I enrolled in Lisa's programme, I was trying to convince senior managers to adopt a particular software application, I remember finishing the delivery and being called by my line manager. He said, 'Toyin, you know your stuff well, but I could sense that you weren't as confident as I know you to be. Toyin, own the stage. There's something that felt like you weren't going as far as I know you can.'

He sensed I wasn't showing myself to be as confident as he knew I was. I thanked him for his feedback, and he wrote the most beautiful recommendation letter when I finished the contract in the organisation.

I remember leaving that day and thinking how much it reminded me of what my Further Maths teacher had said all those many years ago. My manager couldn't figure me out, just as my Further Maths teacher couldn't. That was when I intensified working on myself with Lisa Nichols. We should never stop working on ourselves. Self-development is crucial in the healing of childhood trauma.

Many people have a fear of speaking in public, and it is indeed one of my biggest fears too. But I knew that if I wanted to have an impact, speaking in public was what I needed to do. I decided to go big. I decided to exit this trauma lodged in my body. I went public for the first time to talk about my childhood experiences on 1st February 2020. It was a women's two-day conference event called 'Her Story'. It was soul-satisfying and indeed let me breathe again. It was truly my 'Hush to Roar'.

Top: Me, I registered to attend a Woman's Global Empowerment conference, where I shared my story.

Bottom left: Me, delivering a talk at a mother and daughter event in London.

Bottom right: Me and Lisa Nichols at a Mindvalley self-evolution event in Los Angeles, held from Feb 29th to March 1st 2020

I'd had nerve pain for as long as I could remember. It ran from the back of my head all the way down to my neck. I'd had this for years, and it sounds miraculous (I think it is): I delivered my speech that night, and by the next morning, I had no tension in my neck. I remember mentioning this to almost everyone I saw at the conference on the second day. Each time I wanted to tell them the pain had gone, I'd quickly run my finger down my neck to check if the ache had come back so that I could be sure I wasn't making it up. I am so sure the nerve pain had everything to do with my traumatic experience. I'd always had the problem, and it had become part of me. Even though I still felt the tension, I never went to the doctor. I had so many physical ailments, I was embarrassed about popping in so often. My doctor, although he meant well, would often say with a smile as I walked into his office, 'Mrs Okunuga, what can we do for you this time?'

Public speaking is certainly a therapeutic way to release tensions. I spoke right from my heart, and I didn't hold back. It was as if someone said, 'Toyin, you can breathe deeper now.'

The disappearance of the nerve pain was and still is an incredible revelation about how I didn't know various problems in my body correlated with my childhood experiences. I can't prove any of them do. Still, the more I became communicative about them, the more my healing journey has progressed. Talking about my life experiences is truly like breathing again.

I remember people coming up to me after I'd finished my speech. They said I had inspired them and that felt good. Maya Angelou once said, 'When you learn, teach.' I had learnt how to be me again. I had learnt how to overcome the history of shame. It felt good that I could teach that. Shortly after that event, I did a corporate presentation at work, and it felt good. I was confident, and the presentation piece I delivered got published in our departmental newsletter and rolled out to all other departments. Becoming what I know I've always had inside of me is refreshing.

Today I work as a business analyst/project manager in an international professional services company. I am also the CEO of my business, Hush to Roar, for women who have undergone childhood trauma. I will continue to help and teach women to reach their inner child to live a soul-satisfying life that we all deserve to live.

CHAPTER 19

My Life, My Dance

Having come through my childhood experiences, I know we have it in us to pull through adverse situations. Showing gratitude and re-writing our script allows us to give life all we've got. I learnt to increase in wisdom and recognise that bad things, unfortunately, do happen because life promised us just that. Life.

Our scripts are written once we are born, and our brains appear to be wired nicely, but if they get drastically stripped apart, we re-script our lives in a way that makes it bearable to cope with life's demands. I certainly did that. As children and young adults, we re-script our lives and sometimes dissociate ourselves from the reality of our lives. It is impossible to walk around with so much pain for so long.

As an adult, I have chosen to live full out and no longer allow my past to have a hold on me. It was clear that living an inauthentic life doesn't align with my character. As a result, I would be in constant cognitive dissonance – knowing that my behaviour was not one of authenticity. Still, shame did make me behave inauthentically. I had to resolve and restore this cognitive dissonance. If I didn't, it would continue to manifest itself as stress, regret, shame, embarrassment or feelings of negative self-worth. The effect would be that I'd continuously frustrate all those around me.

When we face adverse childhood experiences and emotional neglect, they make us crave love, externally. We tend to live or 'dance' in other people's worlds to be accepted. We eventually become resentful if love doesn't get reciprocated. It was certainly the case for me. I wanted to be liked, to be loved, but I never for once associated this need with my childhood. I don't think we often do. There is a lot of internalisation that is not seen by many, and some people might say I turned out OK.

I firmly believe that, in addition to my coming to terms with everything, the environment that I grew up in, in Nigeria, didn't leave room for me to even think about how I felt. In a lot of other cases, internalising all we endured as a child and teenager leads to severe mental health conditions.

I exited my body through dissociation. It enabled me to cope better. Everyone has one thing or other that they've gone through, so you internalise everything and then externalise it in ways you are not even aware of. We simply blame the driver that undercuts us for our rage, or we blame our partner for the way they have behaved towards us and so on. But, deep down, we are the ones that have allowed ourselves to react to those situations that way.

Mental illness is a massive part of problems in our society today and most stems from our childhood and teenage experiences. Mental ill-health is the single largest cause of disability in the UK, contributing up to 22.8% of the total burden, compared to 15.9% for cancer and 16.2% for cardiovascular disease. The total economic costs of mental illness in England have been estimated at £105.2 billion each year. These costs include direct costs of services, lost productivity at work and reduced quality of life[1].

Several factors contribute to mental illnesses, and it is often complicated to know what makes up the percentages in the totality of mental diseases. Childhood experiences, no doubt, would be a large contributing factor to this cost.

I have learnt over the years that no one particular event can be trivialised compared to another. And there should be no shame in seeking help for our loved ones to get better if there has been a traumatic event within the family.

A few months ago, I was very excited to read that from September 2020, all pupils in the UK will get taught mental and physical wellbeing. Bold new plans were set out on 25th February 2019 by the former Education Secretary Damian Hinds. He confirmed that from September 2020, pupils of all ages will be taught the new subject – with a focus on promoting the positive link between physical and mental health. To ensure teachers are well prepared ahead of the subject becoming mandatory in 2020, there will be a £6m budget in 2019/20 for a school support package to cover training and resources.[2]

I hope that countries around the world emulate this long-awaited core content that parents, teachers and young people have been crying out to get adopted into schools. The introduction of such a topical aspect to our children's well-being is an initiative that certainly gives me hope for children and young adults.

In recent years I also began to understand more of how my childhood experiences of pain manifested as anger towards others in an erratic way. As I cooked one of my favourite meals, yam and fried egg, I listened to a statement that was made by another one of my spiritual teachers, Dr Wayne Dyer. He said, 'When you squeeze an orange, no matter how much you squeeze it, you will only get orange juice out of it; you can't get apple juice out of it.' I thought, *Hmm, I'm interested to know where this is going*. He then explained further, 'What's inside an orange is what comes out of it.'

I reflected on this statement briefly and the message spoke to me. What was inside of me was anger. And when a colleague or anyone would do anything that was not quite nice or perhaps behave in a way that I thought was inhumane, they squeezed out of me the inner pain I bore, the inner 'don't take me for granted or try to push me about' attitude that I'd lived with for so long.

My mind went back to two of my colleagues, Ena and Geraldine, who I'd worked with around 2012. They always had a measured approach, no matter how annoying or evil-spirited another person was. Even though I would complain about a particular colleague or just someone being nasty towards me or towards others, they would just take little or no notice. They would say things along the lines of, 'Oh well, we know how they are, I wouldn't worry.'

I'd almost feel like screaming and say, 'How can you be so cool about what I'm so furious about?'

I remember on separate occasions talking to each of my colleagues about their childhoods. It wasn't even intentional; we just started talking, and they both, on separate occasions, said how wonderful their childhoods were. Neither of them had a lot by way of money, but they both said their parents were loving and present. I didn't relate what they said to their behaviours, nor did I connect it to mine. But as I listened to the squeezed orange narrative, I said aloud, 'Yep, that was why Geraldine and Ena were always so calm! They have nothing inside them that stirs up anger, hurt or pain, the way I have.'

My two colleagues only had love, kindness and humility in them, so even if a nasty person upset them, their response would be measured. No matter how hard they were 'squeezed', that's what came out of them.

I still reflect on that statement. I make deliberate efforts to make sure that my healing progresses so that when I'm 'squeezed', it's love, joy, humility and empathy that come out of me. I'm aware of the challenge that this poses. When I had negative emotions growing up as a teenager and as an adult, pain, anger, distrust and frustration all spewed out like someone had taken the lid off my juice maker. Unlike an orange, we all have control over what comes out of us when we get 'squeezed'.

There are certainly a lot of exceptions to childhood experiences and outcomes as adults. We all battle through different waves in our lives. There are no guarantees of a pleasant and straightforward adult life, even if you have had a beautiful childhood.

Part of re-defining my life in addition to my 'squeezed' concept was to stop wanting everyone to like me at all costs. I stop expecting people to somehow always 'get me'. I also strive to set healthy boundaries like saying a 'high no' instead of a 'low no'. A high no means a confident, non-wavering one that is polite and firm. The low no would be an agitated, irritable one. I learnt to appreciate me and appreciate my self-worth, no matter what.

It was clear that Royal Mail wasn't going to knock on my door and say, 'Good morning, here you go. You've been through traumatic experiences, but now I have your beautiful life for you.' Nor was Amazon Prime going to send me my life as soon as I said I wanted the one I deserved, 'same-day delivery, please'. Instead of longing for all that I didn't have or what had been taken from me, I had to get the life I wanted.

If we live according to the rules of those we entrusted to keep us safe, and by what got handed to us, we will always dance their dance. In the end, there is only one dance we will dance alone, so we might as well make sure we dance through life. We are now in the driver's seat. Our carers or parents no longer steer the wheel. If the tribe always turns left, but I want to turn right, I know that that tribe no longer serves me. I have to change tribes. I am happy to make mistakes along the way and learn from them.

CHAPTER 20

The Childhood Of A Perpetrator

I never thought I could get to a place in my heart to forgive or empathise with my biological father. Each time I experienced an adverse childhood experience, my trust and reliance on people diminished. Growing up, the more research I did from my late twenties onwards, the more resentment I felt towards my parents. I was growing increasingly resentful towards my family that I believed had failed me. I would also often say, 'Evil strives when good men do nothing,' expecting everyone to have been up in arms for me, and I could never quite see why they weren't climbing mountains to fight my corner. This unforgiving attitude was adding more pain and hurt to me, causing me to feel emotionally drained, even though those who had angered me were getting on with their lives.

It could be likened to driving on the motorway, when a driver suddenly overtakes me dangerously. I could curse all I like and continue the anger when I got home. Still, the driver could be at a party already, having fun, and not having the slightest thought about overtaking me. What a waste of my energy that would be.

The same thing was happening to me through my inability to forgive those I believed had wronged me. This inability to forgive was like drinking poison and expecting the other person to die. I had lived in the past for so long. I just didn't realise that no one had to acknowledge their wrongdoing for me to forgive them.

I started to apply all the spiritual ways of forgiving my father. Sometimes I did think that the teachings weren't referring to a child forgiving their parent for abuse. I found excuses to justify my unforgiving heart. I forgave him intellectually, but that didn't work because my core intentions were those of wanting to live in peace myself, not wanting to accept him as a human being and be loving towards him. The guidance mentioned all types of suffering; I just didn't want to get it. It wasn't working, and I knew I was kidding myself.

The first verse that felt close to my heart growing up as a teenager was the one I discussed in earlier chapters: 1 John 4: 21. 'If anyone says he loves God but hates his brother, he is a liar.' This verse from the Bible was now turning on me. It was becoming a cyclical Karma. I thought deep and realised that this was a universal verse for everyone and every circumstance. As long as I was unforgiving, this verse applied to me too. I went back and forth on my forgiving journey with my father. I was ready to live with my excuses, but I found no satisfaction. It was around late 2018 that I could bring myself to say I was getting to the place where I forgave him. In early 2019, I finally bore no more hate towards him.

If I didn't forgive, I would be giving the world more of what it already had, hate. I realised I couldn't hate, so I must love and forgive. I grew to love God again. I felt God had left me to endure all the hurt and suffering without intervening. But now I knew if I wanted peace and to reach my highest potential, love and forgiveness went hand in hand.

When I moved to my father's house, we went to church every single Sunday. Sometimes we went for a Wednesday gathering of some kind. The Christians in the church often quoted various verses from the Bible. A particular one that was said repeatedly was, 'Jesus said, "I am the way, the truth, and the life. No one comes to the Father except through me".'

I was angry that God said only Christians would go to Heaven, or at least that was my understanding of the verse at the time. I would hear that saying in the church all the time after I started to attend from the age of nine when I got introduced to my Christian father. I thought how unfair it was that I was only fortunate to be a Christian because I was a 'mistake' child. I wondered if that meant all my dearest siblings, mum and stepdad who were Muslims would go to Hell. I also didn't understand why God would let me go through all those sufferings.

I had many doubts about religious beliefs. I was confused, angry and hurt beyond words. I never understood life, and no one provided me with the answers I needed. Some Christians said, 'Now that you know Jesus, go and convert your Muslim family.' It didn't make sense to me. I knew I couldn't convince my Muslim family, and I had doubts myself about Christianity at that point. Besides, Muslims could try to convert Christians too.

In late 2019 I heard of a new book release: *The Universal Christ* by Richard Rohr, a globally recognised ecumenical teacher, American author and spiritual writer. This book gave me a new meaning to life. In the book he argues that when Jesus says he is the 'Way, the truth and the life', he means the way by which all humans and all religions must allow matter and spirit to operate as one. I am convinced that this is indeed the case. I also learnt that I don't need to look for God 'out there'. He is in all of us.

I have grown to link God broadly to my soul because I believe forgiveness is the largeness of soul. Without it, there is no future or creative action – only the repetition of my old stories, remembered hurts, and increasing claims of victimhood.[1]

Learning how to let go of the smaller issues in my life makes it easier to forgive the deep-rooted pain I'd felt and buried for years. I had to invest in myself and read a lot more books, expand my knowledge on the meaning of life and how I could begin to heal from deep inside and not just on the surface. I learnt that for me to reach the highest and most authentic version of myself, I had to do the work. I had to be original and genuine to myself and dance my dance.

It was clear that I had to be rid of the pain that I had and heal from within to be one with my Self. I had to get out all of the hurt that was seated within the deepest parts of my body. It's true that hurting people hurt. It was now up to me to either sort my 'rage body' out or continue to hurt those around me and create a generational toxic curse of hurt. Forgiveness gives us peace, although this, of course, does not excuse people of their acts, nor should it mean that they don't get prosecuted. We know that in a lot of cases, even when the perpetrators get prosecuted, victims are still not satisfied because the truth is that doesn't heal the wounds that are often deep down, wounds that only we can reach.

It was vital to go deep into my healing journey. When we understand others, we will be better informed about their being. As the saying goes, 'You can dig a shallow well and never drink water, or you can dig a deep well and drink forever.' That's how I see my understanding and healing process. I was living a shallow life because I never wanted to go 'there'. As a result of not going to the painful areas within me, I concealed my pain and was living a shallow life. When our recovery is deep, we will thirst no more.

When I bore resentment towards my father, I allowed his hurt to still have a hook on my life. It could be termed as a snake's venom killing me slowly, long after the bite. My energy got depleted. When I was younger, I pretended that my real dad was not my real father. I superimposed my foster dad and my stepdad on to my real dad. He wasn't what I wanted in a daddy. He'd crushed my heart.

Being active in showing empathy was important. When we look into the childhoods of those who have wronged us, if this is at all possible, it might give us a tiny glimpse into why perpetrators do what they do.

Conducting what could be termed as an interview with my father didn't come naturally to me. But I knew I needed to get to the bottom of it for therapeutic healing. I had two goals: to heal and reach a place of genuine forgiveness, and to use my recovery journey to help others on the way to their healing journey.

I wanted to get into his mind. I needed to find out about his childhood to see if there was any correlation to his horrific act. I wanted to help those who were already doing a fantastic job figuring out how, as a society, we can catch the signs early so that the abuse doesn't get carried out in the first place.

It was January 2020. The last time I had spoken to my father was over four years ago. Having come a long way in my healing journey, I was pleased with my progress. I had also forgiven my father to a great extent for his wrongdoing towards me a few years back. Yet I still wanted to find out more about his childhood. Even though he hadn't apologised to me, I had learnt that wrongdoing by someone requires no acknowledgement before forgiveness can take place.

I woke up early on that day and planned to make a phone call to him. I got up to do my morning routine: prayer and meditation, pondering a lot of questions to ask. I wanted to know why he'd done it, why he'd violated me for so many years. I didn't know how to go about asking him, how to start the conversation. I wanted to know if my father had endured extreme adverse childhood experiences that led him to commit sexual abuse towards me. I was almost sure that, even if he had, he wouldn't reveal it to me. He was not of the generation that shared such dark details.

I got my meditation mat and placed it in the living room. I lowered to the ground and tuned in to a forty-minute piece of relaxing music on my mobile. I couldn't relax enough to get into a meditative state. My mind wandered back and forth. I was only entirely in the present for ten minutes or less. My mind was racing. Even though I had forgiven my dad, I still had the opportunity that some people don't have. Some perpetrators who have committed these kinds of acts have died, leaving their victims angry. I was no longer angry. But this was a territory unknown to me. An area that would bring back some difficult memories and I wasn't sure what they would stir up in me.

I just wasn't sure how the conversation would go. But I was getting composed enough to ask him. I was ready to go 'there'.

I went to have a shower and felt freshened. I got dressed and went downstairs to the dining area. No one was at home. I picked up the phone and dialled his number. One part of me wanted him to pick it up, and the other wanted his number to be engaged or for him to just not able to talk. I did get through, and he was available to speak.

'Hello, Dad.'

It felt uncomfortable calling him 'Dad'. I had called him by his initials for years or avoided addressing him altogether. But now I needed to begin with the end in mind. If I was going to get any response from him, I needed to call him 'Dad'.

With a weak and trembling voice as a result of old age, he replied, 'Aah, Toyin, lovely to hear your voice. How are you and the kids and your husband?'

I didn't want to get too chatty. I tried to get to the point, but I also knew that I had to play this cool.

'We are all well, thank you. How are you?'

'I'm fine, thank you.'

He didn't ask why I'd called. He was just happy that I had. Now I had to revert to how I'd planned to go about the questions. After the initial formality of greeting, I went on to say that I'd called to find out a bit about his childhood and that I was asking because we never spoke about things that were upsetting to him. We only ever talked about how brilliant he was in school and how he'd supported his parents while he was working and studying in the UK.

That got him talking for a long time. I thought to myself, *Toyin, you need to take over here and be in control of the conversation.* It reminded me of when I was doing a presentation, and someone wanted to hijack the conversation.

I quickly jumped in and told him that I would like to know a little about his childhood, particularly about the relationship he had with his mum. He laughed and said, 'Ah, ah, is this an interview?' I said it was sort of an interview. I explained to my dad that he never really spoke about his mum and that she had passed away by the time I joined his family in 1985. It was important to me to find out about the relationship he'd had with his mum because I saw his abuse towards me as some kind of response to a sense of 'powerlessness' on his part. I had watched a lot of documentaries on sexual abuse, and there was sometimes a pattern of perpetrators being let down by a female, so I thought asking about my dad's mother could give me some pointers towards his behaviour. Of course, it might have been another woman or something more bizarre that gave rise to his evil act. For some reason, it felt right to ask about his mother.

He told me how his mum had adored him as a child. He said his mum always spoke highly of him and said he was the favourite child and again went into a long conversation. He praised himself as well as his parents.

I asked him to talk to me about any aspect of his relationship with his mum that he got furious about, or any ill-feelings he had as a child and adult. He spoke for another few minutes, reminiscing about his time with her and how he loved her dearly. He got to when she'd passed away, and he said he'd written something on a piece of paper at her graveside. At the end of his note, he wrote, 'Mummy, you didn't say goodbye.'

There was silence.

I said, 'Dad, are you OK?'

He suddenly broke down. I heard him sob uncontrollably; it took him some time before he got composed. It took me by surprise. I had never witnessed this side to my father before. I don't think I had ever seen or heard him cry before that day. For the first time in a very long time, I felt a lot of compassion for him. I could tell he was in a lot of anguish. I had to stay silent and let him sob until he felt able to talk again. I made the inference that he had never completely healed from the passing of his mother. I know we never forget the precious memories we have with our loved ones, but I'd never spoken to an older adult who broke down as a result of talking about their parents. My father was eighty-three when we had the conversation; his mum had died well over forty years before. It threw me off course.

The conversation we had lasted around thirty minutes. I didn't get to ask most of the questions I'd set out to ask, but I witnessed my dad's 'pain body'. The sudden death of his mum was traumatising for him. He, according to him, was his mother's favourite child. He never got to say goodbye to her. She died unexpectedly from tetanus. She was in the village, in Ogun state, my father's home town. He lived in Lagos state and used to travel to see her every month and would take a lot of foodstuffs and money to her. Due to his busy work life, he couldn't go to see her for two consecutive months and instead asked his driver to take money to his mother, so he hadn't seen her for a while when she died. The way his mum died was very different from how his dad passed away. My grandad was over a hundred years old when he died. He held on to dear life until my dad reached him; my grandfather passed away peacefully in his arms.

For that reason, I had compassion for my dad. I empathised. I didn't excuse my father for what he'd done. If I'm honest, I don't even think empathy is befitting here. Because that's the ability to understand and share the feelings of another, and I still couldn't quite understand or share his feelings. I guess I'm not at a higher level of awareness in my spiritual journey yet. But I can say I saw his 'splintered Self'. I did look at it from his frame of reference, so I'll say I empathised with him.

When he finally got composed enough to speak, I told him that I must have unpicked something. I asked my dad if he had carried the pain of losing his mum through to his adult life. He said it had affected him, but it had fizzled out over the years. The only thing he said lasted for years was the fact that he dreamt of her for many years. I asked if he blamed himself for not seeing her before she died or if he blamed his mother. He said he didn't blame himself. I was a bit taken aback that he didn't say he didn't blame his mum, but I wish I'd repeated the question about whether he blamed his mum or not. I didn't ask again, so I can't be sure whether or not he heard me ask specifically about blaming his mum. He went on again to talk about how he'd looked after his parents.

I asked if he'd forgiven himself for the wrongdoings he had done over the years towards other people. He said, 'We will always step on other people's toes'. I did say in my head at that point: *Hmmm, step on people's toes.* He said he had to forgive himself if God already had. I went into saying how forgiving myself is often the hardest thing for me to do. He didn't seem to think it should be a problem. I disagreed but didn't want to dwell on that. That wasn't my objective.

I'd started and was determined to continue with the end in mind. I needed to remain calm. I couldn't prove that the harm he'd done to me was as a result of the sudden death of his mum, and for all I know, it could have been as a result of some other unreconciled pain that caused him to inflict pain on me. I chose my battles carefully. Before I ended the conversation, I explained how he had never asked me about my life before I met him. Explaining how distraught I'd been at leaving Ratby, and subsequently being taken away from my stepdad and half-siblings, I told him that I believed I'd been traumatised by my childhood experiences.

He cut in before I could go any further and said, 'OK, OK, I'm sure you now have the frame of mind to put things into perspective, to re-adjust and re-adjust and look at life in a proper way.'

Those were his exact words. He said he was sure I could forgive and forget and get on with life. It wasn't quite the response I'd expected. I wanted to know how he would respond if I explained to him how I had had many physical ailments as a result of my adverse experiences, but I didn't get that far. I guess I was still expecting an apology. I was slightly (I fibbed, I was very) disappointed that he showed little or no remorse. I sighed and listened to him say how I had made his day and that he'd enjoyed the conversation. I tried to finish the conversation as quickly as possible at that point. I didn't want to stir up negative emotions that I felt rising. I told him to look after himself, and I ended the phone call. I was glad I'd made the phone call even if I didn't quite get the response I wanted. What I got sufficed. I honestly felt free from that moment. I accepted him just the way he was. His answers affirmed everything I'd always known about him. Like most of us, albeit for different reasons, his ego got in the way.

I wish I could say I now know why my father abused me. I will never understand why. We will never know why perpetrators abuse children.

I knew he didn't have it in him to give me what I wanted. For that reason, I rely on higher healing, a pearl of higher wisdom, that makes me understand that it was only one part of his personality (a sub-personality) that did what he did, not his whole character.

Showing empathy allowed me to forgive. I could see my father's 'splintered Self'. Here I refer to how digging deep into his childhood/ mid-adult life revealed to me clearly that every discrepancy between his conscious intention and the emotions that accompanied it pointed directly to a splintered aspect of his 'Self' that required healing.[2]

Having a 'splintered Self' would hold for me too. It was evident that for me to end the cycle of un-forgiveness, hurt and pain, I needed to heal the splintered aspect of my Self. I needed to make all my kind sub-personalities that had been traumatised become whole again. I needed to restore my Self.

How people treat us is their karma; how we react is ours. The empathy, the love that I must show to be free of an imprisoned mind and body is the same love that I feel for those who are undergoing what I endured. It's that empathy, the compassion that I feel when I hear of girls, women, mothers, boys and men who commit suicide due to sexual abuse that they endured for so long. Compassion is the universal love, a universal language and underlying energy that keeps showing itself to me despite my best efforts to resist it. I've held out because it hurts too much when I hear of others who are going through what I did, and I've often felt helpless for them, partly due to the cultural beliefs I explained earlier. Resisting, however, caused severe cognitive dissonance for me.

Although I thought I'd forgiven my father, it was when I interviewed him that I realised I hadn't forgiven him before then. After the interview, I realised there was nothing left for me to hold on to by not showing compassion towards him. I was satisfied and will only ever send him my love and pray that he finds peace. It could have been that I never had the opportunity to interview my father. Would that mean I'd never see things from his frame of reference? No. I would seek and hold on to what I believe to be true, a higher understanding, that it was a part of his splintered Self that he didn't reconcile with and never healed from, that resulted in him hurting me. That would suffice.

The compassion I have is not unique to Christians, Natives, Buddhists, Muslims, Hindus, Taoists, homosexuals, heterosexuals, Blacks or Caucasians, the young or old. It resides in us all.

I know sexual abuse happens worldwide. Doing something about it is satisfying and brings more significant and holistic healing to me. Every child has the right to be out of harm's way. Firstly, they need to be safe in their own home.

Sexual abuse within the family is an area that gets less attention than is needed. From the physical ailments I discussed earlier, it is clear that the abuse of a child can lead to problems with mental and physical health, relationship breakdowns and problems with behaviour. Prevention is the most fundamental form of protection from child sexual abuse. To prevent the abuse of children, in the family environment or otherwise, policy-makers, professionals, parents and adults in local communities need to understand enough about it and know which preventative methods work.[3]

There are a lot of amazing organisations that are fighting to get to the root cause of sexual abuse. I support and follow their work. The Lucy Faithfull Foundation launched Stop It Now! in the UK and Ireland in 2002. It's both a prevention campaign and helpline. The Stop It Now! helpline is an anonymous and confidential service available to anyone with concerns about child sexual abuse, including adults worried about the behaviour of other adults or children and young people; those worried about their own sexual thoughts or behaviour towards children; those with concerns about their online behaviour; friends and relatives of people arrested for sexual offending, including internet offending and any other adult with a concern about child sexual abuse – including survivors and professionals.

It was humbling to read about one of the Stop It Now! callers. He called the helpline asking for help because he had had sexual thoughts towards his friend's teenage daughter. He contacted the helpline numerous times over a four-month period and was given actions to take: implementing immediate child protection measures; using techniques to manage his fantasies; disclosing to his sister who he was close to and continuing to access support from his therapist. By contacting Stop It Now!, he was able to make positive changes to his life.

In 2018/2019 over 5,300 people received advice and support from the Stop It Now! helpline and messaging service.

The NSPCC (National Society for the Prevention of Cruelty to Children), the leading children's charity in the UK, has been running a fantastic education campaign called The Underwear Rule. The rule has the acronym PANTS – Privates are private; Always remember your body belongs to you; No means no; Talking about secrets that upset you; and Speak up, someone can help. A lot of parents use the PANTS rule to educate their children on how to stay safe from as early as three years old. The NSPCC's strategy for young children is to use activity packs called 'Pantasaurus'. The packs show a dinosaur with understandable PANTS statements, not referring to sex or uncomfortable terms that could be difficult to explain. Open discussions about preventing sexual abuse are certainly something that I never had, but I know the exposure in recent years will bring to light this dark and destructive act.

The NSPCC's goal is to make five million children safer by 2021. That's five million children, each with their unique smile, their dreams of what they want to do when they grow up. Their goal is helping protect children today, to prevent abuse tomorrow.

Having spoken to a lot of people in the UK, I realised that the fostering arrangement I had in the 1970s is not a generally known concept. Its existence has only come to surface in recent years. Recently, I remember searching something on Google and stumbling across a heading that said something about foster children. Even though my experience was several decades ago, I have always maintained a keen interest in knowing how the fostering arrangements in the UK stand today.

The Fostering Network in the UK has a broad range of innovative programmes, comprehensive training, resources and celebratory events that have supported, promoted and shared the incredible work of 370 fostering service and 55,000 foster carer members. The Fostering Network also has projects that aim to improve educational outcomes for children and young people in foster care. They have created local academic peer support networks. Seven local authority fostering services joined Fostering Potential and fifty-eight experienced foster carers were recruited and received training to deliver the support networks as education champions.[4]

There is a lot more the Fostering Network is working on, particularly the connection between fostered children and their carers. Some fostered children don't stay in touch with some of the most vital people in their lives. Chief Executive of The Fostering Network Kevin Williams said of a 2019 report, 'Our report shows that all too often, their contact with the former foster family – who they may have lived with for many years – is cut off immediately… Relationships are the golden threads that run through children's lives.'[5]

I'm grateful that I have come through it all. Bringing awareness to fostering organisations, health practitioners and those in strategic positions who can effect change in these areas is more urgent than ever. Collectively we can save a lot more children at risk. After the abuse, when I was twelve, I grew up seeing adults, hoping that someone would read my mind and help me. We have to go to the children. We have to give them tools and implement strategies such as the PANTS initiative for them to be able to come to us. With the correct system in place, I believe child sexual abuse in families will get tackled to a great degree. I am also aware that a radical transformation is the only solution to tackle this hidden and soul-destroying abuse. But I also believe that small steps amount to saving more children.

The compassion I have towards those children that are getting abused right now is equal in different ways to the one I have towards my father. I pray that my dad seeks peace before the end of his days. I will, on the other hand, work to fulfil my passion for stopping sexual abuse within families so that children can live peacefully and reach their full potential before the end of their days too. It's difficult to explain, but I see my empathy as non-dualistic. I now truly forgive my dad, yet I can't sit with myself, knowing that I can help others with my story. I can't explain it. It's not an either/or: my dad or that little girl or boy I'm trying to save. I feel compassion for both of them. I don't need to follow the rules to be loyal to my father as cultural beliefs would want me to do. I know that when we do things because it makes sense to do them, following the rules or beliefs can and should be set aside. I believe in God and know that I have come through all that I have because of God's grace. I know that God has tasked me with this mission. I also believe in the wisdom of Tao, which means that I don't need rules or cultural beliefs to be kind or just. I believe we can be kind to one another because we are all connected.

I also want, just as Oprah said, to help the leaders of tomorrow to take us to the time nobody ever has to say 'MeToo' again.

CHAPTER 21

My Rainbows

Showing gratitude to those who have impacted my life enormously was vital to me. Appreciation for me is a 'win-win'. I believe this has improved my physical and psychological health and made me more empathetic. It has increased my mental strength and improves my relationships with others. My voice was my vehicle for gratitude. Although it's good manners to be appreciative and say thank you, I believe we often forget about those who have been rainbows in our clouds. Their work often goes unnoticed because it is somehow expected of them to be kind. I say not in my case. My foster parents and the village of Ratby, in Leicester, are my angels.

The great Greek philosopher Aristotle said, 'Give me a child until he is seven, and I will show you the man.' There is a lot of truth in that for my life. I couldn't bear to think what my life might have turned out to be if I hadn't started in the precious arms of Mr and Mrs Kind and my wonderful brother and sisters from two months old until I was eight. The start and solid foundation of being immersed in love, deep, genuine care and affection in the first few years of a child's life are crucial in their development. Numerous scientific studies suggest that providing supportive, responsive relationships as early in life as possible can prevent or reverse the damaging effects of toxic stress.[1] What if I'd been placed in the care of foster parents who weren't as loving and still, at eight, taken away to Nigeria, facing all the experiences I did as a child? It would have been like I never knew love. And I genuinely believe that it was because I had tasted love before that I was able to navigate my way through the perils that I faced. I'm grateful that I got placed in the Kinds' care. I'm grateful to my darling sister, Carolyn, for insisting that Mum Kind responded to the advert placed about me.

I know a lot of people, unfortunately, have only ever known pain. I am confident that if help is sought early on in life, recovery can and will certainly happen. Research shows how much our brain can condition and recondition itself throughout our lifetime, and we can train our minds to think positively, thereby increasing our overall mental wellbeing. It may not be easy, and it might take sustained effort, but we can 'remodel' our brains at any age in ways that can help us to function better.[1]

Once I reconnected with Ratby village on Facebook, I wanted to publish my expression of gratitude. I reached out to the *Leicester Mercury* newspaper[2] to get my story of fostering out in the open for the entire village to see and to share my appreciation of the love I was shown. It was published both online and in print. This was refreshing, and it was very gratifying and therapeutic too. They indeed were my rainbows. My message was simple: 'I just want to say thank-you.'

I have been for so long in the darkness, but as I move towards the light, although it is a long and bittersweet journey, I am grateful. I feel no shame for who I am. We can, I believe, rise through it all. I learnt to laugh again and laugh, I do! I surround myself with those that will make me laugh. I have belly laughs, and it comes right from my soul.

I firmly believe that time doesn't heal us. We recover over time as we take intentional and deliberate steps. It takes time but becomes less painful only if we take intentional healing measures. If I hadn't started my recovery journey, the pain would simply be deep-rooted and untouched but would undoubtedly get externalised through my actions. Despite the horrific hurt and pain of betrayal, we face them all. I have a lot of blessings in my life. And for that reason, I am grateful and feel no shame.

There is pride in courage, there is pride in persistence and pride in survival. Even as we feel the pain of betrayal, when we look to the sun,

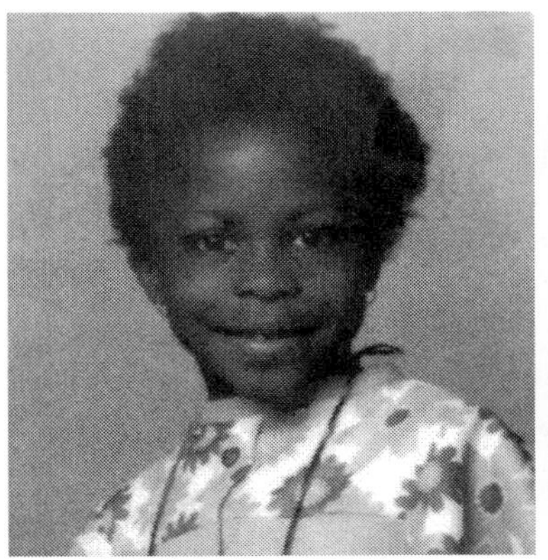

I only recently discovered I was only black girl in villag

WOMAN SUDDENLY SPLIT FROM FOSTER PARENTS REMEMBERS HER TIME IN COUNTY

Top left: Me at seven years old.
Top right: Me with mum and dad Kind.
Bottom left: grandmum and grandad Kind.
Bottom right: Article in the Leicester Mercury.

it's still shining. It's still shining on all of us and does not discriminate. I think of the sun as my friend, from Martin Shaw Woods. I think of my forest friends, and how they all would love me to be free-spirit-minded and to open my heart to all opportunities that are out there and feel no bitterness.

We all have our stories, and none should get downplayed. All our experiences are unique, and I am sure everyone's story will resonate with someone out there, inspire and even transform another's life.

Coming through my own experiences, I smile when I think of my fun days. I am so grateful to have had life experiences with so many people. The many siblings that I have are an immeasurable blessing. I'm grateful for all my experiences and own all of them.

We can't undo the past, but we can choose to work on ourselves. We are not alone. We can come through the horrifying history that some of us have endured, and accept that we did go through those adverse experiences. When we stand on top of our stories instead of swimming in them, we will empathise with those who might be going through adverse childhood experiences today.

Thank you all for taking the time to travel with me. The agony of an untold story is unbearable. I am victorious, I am a survivor; we are all survivors of our childhood experiences, and we can learn from every single one of them. For that reason, we need not be ashamed, but be grateful.

Above: My sweet sis Carolyn, she loved nature, she loved birds, and she fed them, and would watch them fly away to be free. I feel as free as a bird. I miss you Carolyn! My mind is no longer caged.

Little did you know that your persistence for mum to respond to the advert about me, marked the day I would feel unconditional love, tenderness and the emotional stability that would pull me through all the perils I faced.

Thank you sis! I miss you!

Acknowledgements

The writing of this book was by no means a solo act. I truly believe that I was sent a lot of extraordinary people to help me in the journey of my book, from the beginning to the end. All those who played significant roles in my life made this book a reality. I am eternally grateful to those who kept me motivated and determined throughout. Without them all, my life would not be what it has become and this book wouldn't exist:

Children
First and foremost, I'd like to thank my two most adorable cheerleaders. My children - Thank you for being the most intelligent and uplifting children I could ever wish for. Without your full support, I don't think I would have finished writing this book. Thank you for believing in me and saying, 'Go for it, Mum, we are proud of you, you are inspirational.' You truly made me breathe again.

Family
The Kinds:
Mrs Shirley Kind – Mum, I love you! God sent you to me! I have so much to say, but, paradoxically, I have no words! I had no idea how much you meant to me until I started writing my book. You are my rainbow! And I love you more than any words can express in writing.

Andrew Kind – My darling bros. Thank you for being part of my life journey. Thanks for being available to fill in the gaps about how I was when I was with you in Ratby. I had forgotten some details but you took the time to chat with me for ages. Thank you for being generous with your time.

Paula Buckley – My sis. Thank you for all your love and the chats we had during the writing of my book. Thinking of you and how loving you were to me brought up so many emotions for me. I just thank you for being the closest sister who was always there to tell me how I was with you as a baby and growing up with you. I love you, Sis.

Julie Warren – My big sis. Thank you for being a vital aspect of my life. Thank you for providing me with everything I asked for when I was writing this book. You are my blessing, you have been my cheerleader and I love you for being available whenever I needed to get in touch.

Natalie Sperry – My darling niece! You had the greatest mum ever! Carolyn would have been so proud of you and David with everything you have accomplished. Thanks for telling me about how much Carolyn spoke about me before I returned to the UK and sharing more pictures of me and Carolyn – It means so much to me. I love you!

My birth mum – Mum, thank you for providing me with the information to fill the gaps in my book-writing. Thank you for loving me the way you know how and for ringing me constantly even when I sometimes fell short in ringing as much as you wanted me to.

To my siblings, thank you all for showing your support in different ways and for reaching out during my book-writing journey.

Teachers

Dr Mrs Adefolaju Falade. My English teacher – You gave me the sense of what happiness and fulfilment really meant when I scored highly in my English test. It boosted my morale; you had the best words to lift my spirit when I needed to hear it most.

Mr Azubuike Oguine. My Further Maths teacher – You were the single most enlightening teacher in my life. You were the one who gave me the light bulb moment in my life. You were one of the most humbling, gentle and caring teachers who went beyond their job description. We need more of you! Thank you!

Virtual teachers

Lisa Nicholls – Thank you for showing me through your thorough and well-thought-out courses that my voice and story matters. Thank you for being one of the early contributors in my life that made it known to me that my story is not to be hidden and that shame should have no place. Thank you for helping me find the courage to be vulnerable. Thank you, Lisa. Because of you, I haven't needed to seek out a therapist for my recovery. I dug deep inside and all I needed was inside me.

Richard Rohr – I had no real understanding of my faith and didn't know how to put in words all my reasoning. You conveyed it to me in plain English. When I read your book, The Universal Christ, it was a pivotal moment for me. I was able to explain things in my book in a cohesive manner. Thank you.

Gary Zukav – Your inspirational book, *The Seat of the Soul*, was what made me truly understand 'authentic power' and 'splintered Self'. Your book was what made my healing journey of forgiveness become as progressive and complete as it is today. I could only truly forgive when I read the meaning of what it meant to forgive. Thank you!

Eckhart Tolle – Your teachings have been the enlightenment and enrichment to my forgiveness journey. Without me truly having the mindset and wisdom to forgive those I believe wronged me, I would not have been able to write my book. There would have been no victory in writing without a heart of forgiveness. Your inspirational and God-given words enabled me to write my book in the complete and inspiring way that I needed to convey to my readers.

Mentors

Michelle Obama – Thank you for writing your memoir, *Becoming*. This book consolidated my decision to come out with my story. Your words and authenticity reiterated that fact that using my voice is powerful. Thank you!

Oprah Winfrey – Because of your teachings, I knew I was not alone. Through your personal experience, I found the courage to tell my truth, knowing that by speaking about my story I would let my own children understand who their mum really is and for them to understand where I'm coming from in all my endeavours. You sought out the best teachers to come on your show. Your wisdom – of asking the questions that you did – made it possible for me to truly understand how to convey my message in my book. Thank you, Oprah.

Authors

Stephen Covey – When I read your book so many years ago, the single most important message that I took from it has been my reference point today. It has helped me in my journey to recovery and my story-telling. 'Begin with the end in mind' has been the golden key to all the doors that have been opening for me. Thank you.

Bessel Van Der Kolk – When I read your book I was sure you must have met me and asked about my life story! Your book was ground-breaking! Your book, *The Body Keeps The Score*, is the book that brought me to my knees. I sobbed and raised my head to the ceiling and said, 'Toyin, your behaviour is normal, everything you went through as a child was a contributing factor to your behaviour as an adult. It's OK, you're OK, now begin to heal and live the life you deserve.' Thank you, Bessel Van Der Kolk!

Friends

Leicester, Ratby:

Kerry Spiers – My Ratby school bestie! Thanks for filling in some gaps when I needed to remember what we both got up to during our childhood days. Thanks for being a part of my story – that made it complete – and contributing to my life; the most pleasant and most memorable days as a child. Thank you, Kerry!

Joanne Murfin – Thank you for being my booster friend in my book journey. Thank you for being in my book as a dear friend back in Ratby. You have been a friend that has given me the encouragement to keep going and have been an active contributor to the choices of my book cover design, blurb and other essential materials needed for the overall success of my book. Thank you!

Tracey Hamilton – Thank you for being part of my book as a close friend back in Ratby. Thanks for being with me on my writing journey and giving me praise and urging me to keep going. Thank you!

Command secondary school:

Fisayo Olaleye – You never gave up on me, even when I'd want to be left alone and not ring you back when you'd ring me time and time again. You always somehow 'got me'. You have always been there as a true friend, as my best friend. The encouragement you gave me throughout my book-writing has been soul-satisfying. You showed me what a best friend truly means. I love you, Fifi!

Pere Owota – You have given me your time to be part of an active contributor in my book journey. You were one of the first to say the story in me was ready to be born! And since then you have taken on the book-writing journey as your own. Your input has been immeasurable. Thank you, Pere!

Tunde Ogunleye – You have been my right-hand buddy! You have been one of the most amazing friends in my life. You made me see I was suffering a 'disease to please' and woke me up in ways that allowed me to convey my message clearly. You have been my friend, my brother, my confidant, my editor and just about everything needed in a friend. Your nickname, 'experience', is truly befitting! Tunde, I appreciate you!

Adekemi Babarinde – Thank you for being one of the most inspiring and authentic besties ever! You always give me the best of you! I could count on you all through my book-writing and elsewhere. You didn't say things just to make me feel good, you said things that would lift my book to higher levels. You are truly a woman of inspiration! Thanks, Kemi! I love you, Sis!

Femi Okegbenro – You have been one of my most incredible, uplifting friends! You have always been my supporter in everything I've set out to do since I intensified my healing process. You always say, 'Toyin, just do it! Go for it.' You have always been an active listener when I needed someone to talk to. Femi, thank you!

Uduak Akpabio – My prof! You are reliable, dependable and always on point with your timings! You are a true friend and have made my book journey complete. Thank you, Uddy!

Vera Ohanele Tokbe – My dearest bestie! Thank you for being a true and reliable friend to me! Thanks for being a cheerleader and being selfless in the time you dedicated to being one of my advance readers. Thanks for always being there! I love you, Sis.

David Nkechukwume Innocent – My pastor! You have been one of my most amazing friends! Your words and prayer points have been soul-soothing. Your middle name 'Nkechukwume', meaning 'Crafted by God', is truly befitting. The in-depth care and prayers throughout my writing journey has been reassuring and has consolidated my courage to keep going. Thank you! I really appreciate you!

Mashim Owoborode – You have been one of my most inspiring and comforting friends ever! Thank you for being a listening ear, for giving advice throughout my book-writing journey and for being authentic in the analysis of the book. Thanks, Mashim!

Blaise Zirra – Thank you for being part of my story and making my book journey complete. You were a gentle and true friend who always took the time to explain things to me over and over again when I could never seem to grasp things very well. Thank you for your soothing and calm words of encouragement on Facebook. Thank you, Blaise!

Akinfe Akinwale – My buddy and bestie from back then. Thanks for always finding the time to teach me until I understand. Thanks for being my cheerleader towards the final aspect of my writing journey. Thank you!

Koya Clement Ahmiegbe – Thank you for being one of my advance copy readers and taking time to go through all the details with an objective mind and sharing your true thoughts on all aspects of the book. Thank you!

Polytechnic of Ilaro:

Adetutu Keshinro – My most-loving bestie and sister! You kept me safe and took the most vital lifesaving steps that kept me alive! I have no words. Without you, I might not be here to have written my book. Tutu, I love you from the bottom of my heart.

London:

Toyin Badmus Funsho – Thank you for being my bestie! You have been my rock for almost twenty-five years! You have cheered me on and said words that have been soothing and encouraged me to keep going in my book-writing journey. Toyin, I love you!

Florence Yemi Benjamin – My sister, thank you for giving me the most God-lifting words that have seen me through my story-telling journey. Thank you for your ever-generous words of comfort and sisterly love when I needed them most.

Ena Miller – Thank you for all your encouragement along the way; you've always been like a big sister to me. Your humility, yet bold and confident approach to life has always been a source of reference to me. Your advice over the past eighteen years that we have known each other, since we met at work, has been soul-gratifying, thank you.

Basildon:
Claire Marie – Thank you for being a wonderful friend and neighbour and one of my advance readers and for giving your honest review on the book. Thanks also for asking how I'm getting on with it along the way and being around when I needed to pop over to you to have a chat! Thanks, Claire!

Tabitha Mathiu – Thank you for cheering me on throughout my writing journey, thanks for always being a friend that I could ring up and hang out with. Thank you, Tabitha!

Personal growth community

Speak and Inspire:
Lee Immerzeel
Lynda Langusch
Mel Forbes
Sanna Edlund
Gao Motsemme
Blossom Murphy
Micheal Earle
Joel Mwansa
Karen Lowe

Thank you all for encouraging me in my book journey and boosting me with so much confidence; the confidence that I sometimes doubted, you reinforced with your inspirational words and blessings. Thank you, all!

Ignite Your Speaking:
Cheryl Verret – Thank you for being part of the 'Hush to Roar' group and answering the various questions that I asked.

Bisi Braimah – Thank you for being a 'full-on' advance reader of the book. You asked questions to clarify various aspects and ensured that my message came across in a coherent manner. Thank you!

The publishing team

Emee Vida Estacio – Your book-writing company, Self Made Publishing Made Easy, helped me with the initial steps I needed to take to dip my toes in an unfamiliar territory. Your easily explained process revealed a side to me that I never thought I'd see. It made me realise that the book I wrote was always in me. Your step-by-step approach made it easy to dive into telling my story without 'writers' block'. Thanks, Emee!

Bethany Wright – Developmental and copy-editor. Your in-depth knowledge ensured that my writing stayed on point and you took the time to explore all areas to ensure the structure and arrangement of different aspects to my story flowed well and stayed consistent. Thanks for your patience.

Paul Palmer-Edwards – Book and cover designer. You took on my project like we had known each other for years! You were patient with all my book cover swapping and went above and beyond what I expected from a designer. Thank you for designing the cover exactly how I felt it should be; without me even saying a word to you! Thanks, Paul, you're a genius.

Nicky Lovick – Proofreader. I truly believe I don't go out to get people, they come to me. I know you came to me because you worked on my book as if it was your 'pet project'. You exceeded my expectations and I feel you're my sister! Thank you, Nicky.

In Loving Memory

Carolyn Sperry – I will for ever be your baby sis. I miss you so much. You were the reason for my story and I know you are with the angels, watching down on me. You were the most generous and kind-hearted being I have ever known. You were in my thoughts every step of my writing journey. The emotion that writing this book brought up was gratitude every time I thought of you. You always had the right words to say to me and you had a way to keep me going as I wrote this book. I love and miss you, Carolyn! I can't say any more, I really miss you!

Grandma and Grandpa Kind – You were my added 'security blanket'. The hugs; the wisdom you shared and endless fun times we had together were no doubt major contributing factors giving me a chance and not to go down a path of self-destruction. I tasted love and I had the emotional stability as a cushion from you both. I love and miss you both dearly.

Mr Ernest Kind – You took me in and didn't care what anyone said or thought of having a black baby. Dad, you left us on Carolyn's birthday on the 17th December 2019. I know you are together now. I miss you, Dad! Your name says it all! You lived your name and I felt you throughout my book-writing journey. 'Com'n, me duck!' was what I kept hearing and I was in flow. Dad, you were a rare gem! I love and miss you so much.

My step-dad – Dad, I miss you and I'm so sorry I drifted away from you when I did. I knew you were hurting just as much as I was. I'll always be your little girl! You loved me and were heartbroken when I got taken away from you. I was devastated. I miss you, Dad!

Maya Angelou – Your wisdom was healing to me. Your poems gave me renewed strength and kept me in motion. Because of your words of wisdom, I didn't see a therapist. Thank you, Maya!

Dr Wayne Dyer – Your teachings have been one of the most practical and realistic ways for me to explain, fully, my behaviours and how what is in me is what was coming out of me. The 'squeezed orange' concept was one of the most wonderful concepts that gave me meaning and allowed me to explain in my writing. Thank you! Because of your books and online tutorials, I didn't seek therapy or counselling for my healing process.

Notes

Chapter 11: The Rage Body
1. Good Therapy – Internal Family Systems https://www.goodtherapy.org/learn-about-therapy/types/internal-family-systems-therapy

Chapter 13: Inner Child Healing Begins
1. Laguipo, AngelaBetsaida B, 'Is Dancing Good for the Brain?', https://www.news-medical.net/health/Is-Dancing-Good-for-the-Brain.aspx#:~:text=Dancing%20improves%20brain%20function%20and,of%20dementia%20among%20the%20participants

Chapter 14: Being Silenced
1. Solnit, Rebecca, 'Silence and powerlessness go hand in hand – women's voices must be heard', *Guardian*, 8th March 2017, https://www.theguardian.com/commentisfree/2017/mar/08/silence-powerlessness-womens-voices-rebecca-solnit

Chapter 16: Helping You Help Us
1. British Tinnitus Association, https://www.tinnitus.org.uk/tinnitus-and-stress

2. Murphy, Colleen, 'Arthritis May Be Linked to Childhood Trauma', https://www.consultant360.com/exclusive/rheumatology/pediatrics/arthritis-may-be-linked-childhood-trauma

3. Sigurdadottir, Sigrun and Sigridur Halldorsdottir, 'Screaming Body and Silent Healthcare Providers: A Case Study with a Childhood Sexual Abuse Survivor', https://www.mdpi.com/1660-4601/15/1/94/htm

4. Cleveland Clinic, 'How to help children recover and thrive after adversity', https://health.clevelandclinic.org/childhood-traumas-lasting-effects-on-mental-and-physical-health/

5. Ibid

6. Rascon, Gaby, 'What is Brain Fog? Symptoms & Treatment Options', 16th July 2019, https://www.steadymd.com/2019/07/16/brain-fog/

7. IHMRI, 'Links between gestational diabetes and childhood trauma', 1st August 2019, https://www.ihmri.org.au/links-between-gestational-diabetes-and-childhood-trauma/

Chapter 17: Becoming One With Self
1. McLeod, Saul, 'Maslow's Hierarchy of Needs', Simply Psychology, updated 20th March, 2020, https://www.simplypsychology.org/maslow.html

2. IFS Institute, "'What is Internal Family Systems?/', https://ifs-institute.com/

3. Elium, Don, '8 Cs of Self', http://www.don-elium-psychotherapy.com/8-cs-of-self

4. Schwartz, Richard C., 'Trauma & The Internal Family Systems Model: Releasing Personal & Legacy Burdens', https://ifs-institute.com/news-events/workshops/132

5. Zukav, Gary, *Seat of the Soul*, rev. ed. London: Rider, 2015.

Chapter 18: Hush To Roar

1. NHS EDUCATION FOR SCOTLAND Transforming Psychological Trauma, https://www.nes.scot.nhs.uk/media/3971582/nationaltraumatrainingframework.pdf

2. Nichols, Lisa, 'Speak and Inspire', https://www.mindvalley.com/speak

Chapter 19: My Life, My Dance

1. Department of Health, 'No Health without Mental Health', https://assets.publishing.service.gov.uk/government/uploads/system/uploads/attachment_data/file/215808/dh_123993.pdf

2. Department for Education, 'All pupils to be taught about mental and physical wellbeing in schools from 2020', https://www.fenews.co.uk/press-releases/26128-all-pupils-to-be-taught-about-mental-and-physical-wellbeing-in-schools-from-2020

Chapter 20: The Childhood of a Perpetrator

1. Rohr, Richard, *The Universal Christ*, p.72. London: SPCK Publishing, 2019.

2. Zukav, Gary, *Seat of the Soul*, rev. ed. London: Rider, 2015.

3. NSPCC, https://www.nspcc.org.uk/about-us/performance-plans-strategy/

4. The Fostering Network, 'Annual Review for the year ended 31 March 2019', https://www.thefosteringnetwork.org.uk/sites/www.fostering.net/files/content/annualreview2018-19.pdf

5. The Fostering Network, 'Fostered children's important relationships severed', 12th November 2019, https://www.thefosteringnetwork.org.uk/news/2019/fostered-childrens-important-relationships-severed

Chapter 21: My Rainbows

1. Ackerman, Courtney E. 'What is Neuroplasticity? A Psychologist Explains [+14 Exercises]'. 28th April 2020. https://positivepsychology.com/neuroplasticity/

2. https://www.leicestermercury.co.uk/news/leicester-news/the-only-black-girl-village-3890388

Thank you for reading, I hope you liked the story. If you did enjoy the book or find it useful, please could you leave a review on the site where you bought it.

To receive regular, relevant information on childhood trauma and recovery, please visit my website **www.hushtoroar.com**

You can also follow me on:

Facebook: Toyin Balogun Okunuga

Instagram: @toyin_b_okunuga4/

Twitter: @ToyinOkunuga1

Printed in Great Britain
by Amazon